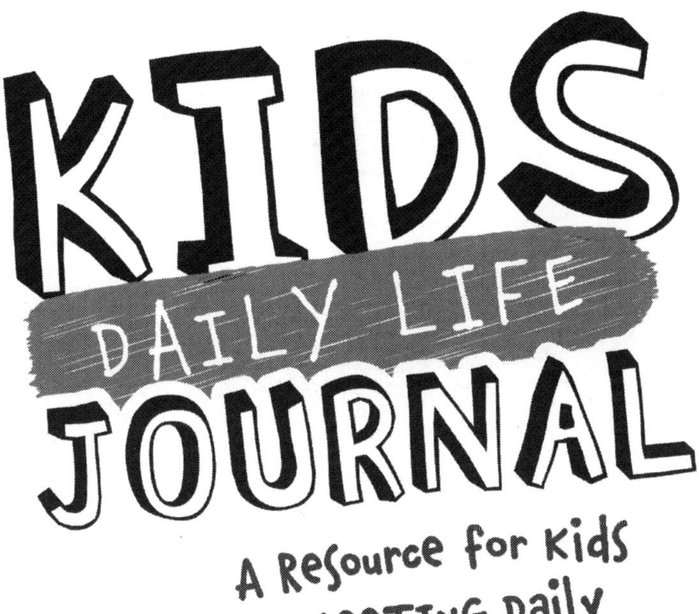

A Resource for Kids Meeting Daily with God

Written by

Dale Evrist, Joel Evrist, and Donna Phillips

Cover illustration by Salmos del Villar
Layout design by Sarah Siegand
Interior original artwork by Madi Goodside,
Salmos del Villar and Jordyn Byers

Printed in the United States of America.
ISBN: 9781710592429

Table of CONTENTS

Introduction

3 MAIN PLACES

THE BIBLE TEACHES

that there are three main places that we are to spend our time in prayer and praise to God and in serving others: The Secret Place, The Gathering Place and The Public Place. It is important that we know where we are to go and what we are to do to live our lives for the glory of God and the good of others.

The Kids Daily Life Journal will help you to focus on the Secret Place as you spend time in prayer and praise to the Lord and journal about what God is showing you in His Word and by His Spirit.

1 The Secret Place

☆ Read Matthew 6:6

In the Secret Place we come to be alone with God the Father and Jesus the Son by the leading of the Holy Spirit. This is where we receive direction for our day and grow in a personal relationship with God.

☆ Read Matthew 18:18-20

In the Gathering Place we come together with God's people to serve one another, directed by God's Word and His Holy Spirit.

3 The Public Place

☆ Read Acts 2:46-47

In the Public Place we reach neighbors, nations and generations with the good news of Jesus Christ's love and power.

LESSON 1

Welcome to THE SECRET PLACE

1 WELCOME TO THE SECRET PLACE

What is the Secret Place?

☆ **Read Matthew 6:6**

When Jesus came to earth, He called people to prayerfully seek the Heavenly Father in the Secret Place. The Secret Place is a place where we can be alone with God. The Secret Place is a place we meet every day with God, rather than a place we visit from time to time. This special place is where we listen, study and meditate on the Scriptures, pray, praise and journal. (☆ **Read Psalm 5:1-3.**)

Why Should I Be in the Secret Place?

We have been created on purpose for purpose – which is to know God forever. In the Old Testament, every commandment declares who God is and draws us to know Him more deeply. In the New Testament, Jesus' life, death and victorious resurrection gives us a new and living way to know God. One day in the future when every nation has heard the gospel, Jesus will return, and we will be with Him forever. Until that day, we can grow in knowing Him through the Secret Place. (☆ **Read Psalm 27:4-5.**)

How Do I Find My Secret Place?

Jesus never commands us to do what He has not already done. He always found a personal place to seek God and calls us to do the same. So, your Secret Place is really any place you can be alone with God. The most important thing in finding your Secret Place is to pray and ask God when and where He wants you to meet with Him each day. (☆ **Read Mark 1:35.**)

LESSON 2

How to use your DAILY LIFE JOURNAL in

2

HOW TO USE YOUR DAILY LIFE JOURNAL IN THE SECRET PLACE

Your Kids Daily Life Journal will help you grow in your relationship with the Father, the Son and the Holy Spirit in the Secret Place every day. The Holy Spirit is ready to lead you to love, look, listen, learn and live.

LOVE

Read Mark 12:29-31

The Bible says that God sent His only Son, Jesus, to make us His sons and daughters because He loves us. Begin each time in the Secret Place by asking Jesus to fill you freshly with His Holy Spirit and with His love. As a son or daughter of the Father, you can boldly come to God each and every day in prayer for yourself, your family, your friends and those in the world.

LOOK

☆ Read Psalm 63:1-2

The Secret Place is to help you to learn more of God's Word, will and ways. Look to God and make Him the focus of your prayers and praise. Look into the Word of God to see what it says, what it means and what to do.

LISTEN

☆ Read John 16:13

Listening in the Secret Place will help you to hear what God is saying. Like a student who listens closely to a teacher, listen closely to the Holy Spirit's voice while studying the Word, praying, praising and journaling.

LEARN

☆ Read 2 Timothy 2:15

Using a Bible in an easy-to-understand translation and the Walking Through the Word Daily Reading and Study Guide in your Kids Daily Life Journal, ask the Holy Spirit to teach you new things every day from His Word. Using the journal pages, write down what the scripture says, what the scripture means, and what you will do to obey the scripture.

Take your Kids Daily Life Journal with you wherever you go to help you remember what you have heard and what you have written down. Live out what you have received in the Secret Place when you are with others in the Gathering Place and the Public Place.

Lesson 3

How to walk Through the Word in

3 HOW TO WALK THROUGH THE WORD IN THE SECRET PLACE

Read 2 Timothy 3:16-17

As you walk through the Word using the Walking Through the Word Daily Reading and Study Guide included in your Kids Daily Life Journal, the following guidelines will help you better understand what each passage of scripture is saying, what it means, and what to do with what you've learned.

What Does It Say?

As you read each scripture passage, ask the question, "What does it say?" This will help you to have a better understanding of what you have read. Write down the things that stand out to you.

What Does It Mean?

After you have asked the question, "What does it say?", then ask the question, "What does it mean?" One of the ways you can find out more about what it means in the time and place it was written is to use a good study Bible. If you don't have a good study Bible, ask someone older than you to help you understand more about what the passage means.

What Will I Do?

As you discover what the scripture passage says and means, write down what you have learned. Then, think about the scripture passage and speak it out repeatedly. This will help you to remember the scripture and put it into daily practice.

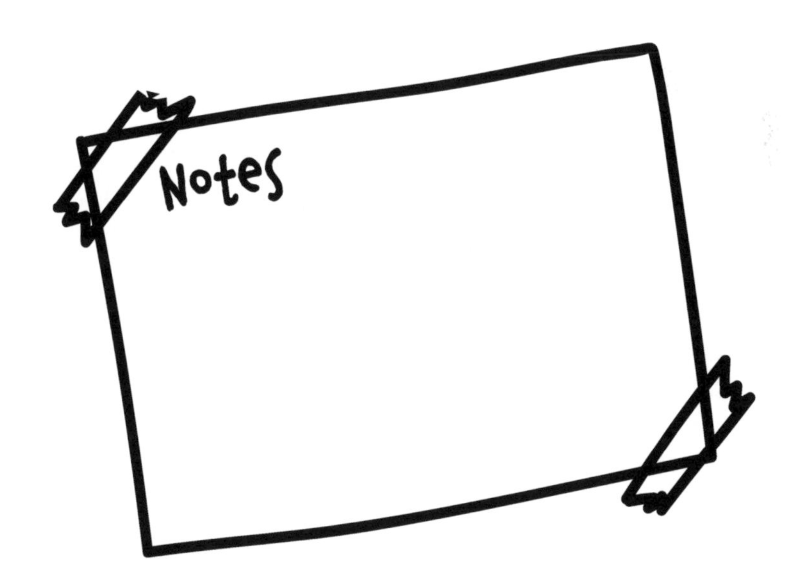

Lesson 4

How to Pray in

HOW TO PRAY IN THE SECRET PLACE

Read Matthew 6:9-13[1]

Jesus' disciples asked Him to teach them how to pray and what to pray. Jesus gave them a way to pray that is also a guide to help you when you pray in the Secret Place. The following will help you to pray the way Jesus taught.

"Our Father in heaven,"

You are a child of God; He created you! You can be at peace knowing that He is your Heavenly Father who cares for you and never leaves you.

[1]The Scripture passage listed in this section is taken from The Christian Standard Bible®.

"Your Name be honored as holy."

We choose to keep God's name separate from any other name because He is honored and holy. The Bible gives us many different names of God that tell us more about who He is and what He's like. Here are some of His names:

Names of God

El Elyon | "God Most High"

(☆ Read Genesis 14:18)

El Shaddai | "God Almighty"

(☆ Read Genesis 17:1)

Yahweh Jireh | "The Lord Will Provide"

(☆ Read Genesis 22:14)

Yahweh Rophe | "The Lord Who Heals"

(☆ Read Exodus 15:26)

Yahweh Shalom | "The Lord Is Peace"

(☆ Read Judges 6:24)

"your kingdom come. your will be done on earth as it is in heaven."

Pray for things to be the way God wants them to be:

In my family

In my city

In my country

In my world

"Give us today our daily bread."

Ask God to give you all you need for each day.
You can depend on Him for everything!

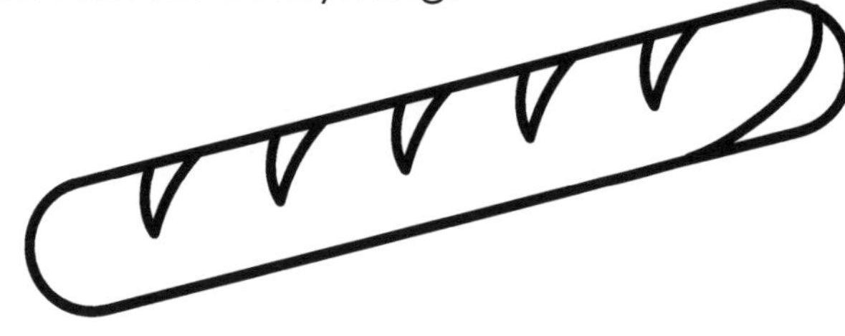

"And forgive us our debts, as we also have forgiven our debtors."

When we confess (tell) our sin to God, we are saying, "I did it." Then we turn away from our sin and turn towards God, which is called repentance. God promises to forgive our sins if we confess and repent of them. (☆ **Read 1 John 1:9.**)

Just as God has forgiven us, we need to forgive others when they sin against us. Be quick to forgive! (☆ **Read Mark 11:25-26.**)

"And do not bring us into temptation, but deliver us from the evil one."

Temptation is not sin. Even Jesus was tempted! (☆ **Read Matthew 4:1-11.**) The Bible says that when we are tempted to sin, God will provide a way for us to say "no" to the temptation so that we don't sin, and He will keep giving us strength as we choose to say "no" to sin. (☆ **Read 1 Corinthians 10:13.**)

Where and when are you tempted to sin? Talk to God about those times and ask for His help to say "no" to sin.

PRAYER GUIDE

N
W E
S

These QUESTIONS ☞ WILL HELP YOU as you PRAY

What things can you thank God for?

WHAT THINGS DO YOU NEED TO TRUST GOD FOR TODAY?

Have you seen God answer your prayers?

What are your prayer requests? Write them down!

Lesson 5

How to PRAISE in

5 HOW TO PRAISE IN THE SECRET PLACE

Read Psalm 5:1-3

The Secret Place isn't necessarily a quiet place. It may be quiet at times, but it's also to be a place where we use our voice to praise God for who He is and what He has done. Praise in the Secret Place should begin in the morning. (**Read Psalm 5:1-3.**) Throughout the Scriptures, people are seen as beginning the day by seeking God. (**Read Mark 1:35.**) Beginning the day with praise helps you to honor God in everything.

Praise in Speaking

King David said that praise should be spoken from grateful lips. (**Read Psalm 63:3-6.**) The term bless means to recognize that all blessings in life come from God. Our God is worthy to be praised every day, in every way throughout the day.

Praise in Singing

Many times in the Bible we are told to express our praise to God with singing. These can be songs that are written and well known or songs that simply flow from our hearts. We are to serve the Lord with joy for all the good things He has done for us and come before Him with singing that is full of love and thankfulness. (☆ Read Psalm 100:1-5.)

Praise in Moving

Dancing before the Lord is a wonderful way to express our praise to Him. (☆ Read Psalm 149:1-4.) We can do it through steps and movements that are planned and rehearsed or just by moving from side-to-side, leaping for joy or making any movement that involves our whole self in praise. Lifting our hands, clapping our hands and waving our hands are also ways to be free and open in offering praise to our great God.

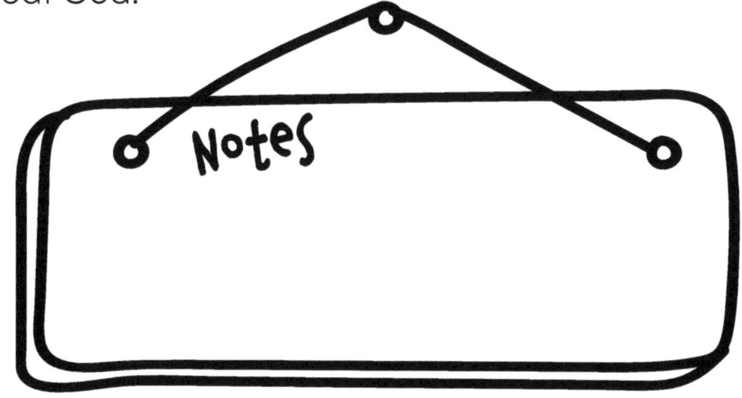

LESSON 6

HOW TO JOURNAL YOUR JOURNEY IN

6 HOW TO JOURNAL YOUR JOURNEY IN THE SECRET PLACE

☆ Read Habakkuk 2:1-4

In the Old Testament, Habakkuk committed to journal his journey with God and because he did this, he and others received God's direction for their lives.

In the New Testament, Luke writes details of the life and ministry of Jesus and His followers. **(☆ Read Luke 1:3-4.)** Because he wrote and journaled well, we have a guidebook on how to follow Jesus each day.

Journal Your Journey Daily

Every day is a new opportunity to write down what God is showing you in His Word and how you are growing in your relationship with Him. Try not to miss a day of journaling so that you can remember the work of God in your life. **(☆ Read Lamentations 3:22-23.)**

Journal Your Journey in Writing

Write down the details of what God is saying and doing each day as you spend time in the Secret Place. This will help you to grow strong in your Lord and Savior Jesus Christ. **(☆ Read 2 Peter 3:18.)**

Journal Your Journey in Pictures

Your journaling is not to be dull. Let your journaling be filled with words and pictures of life and love that show what God is doing in and through you. **(☆ Read 2 Corinthians 3:17–18.)**

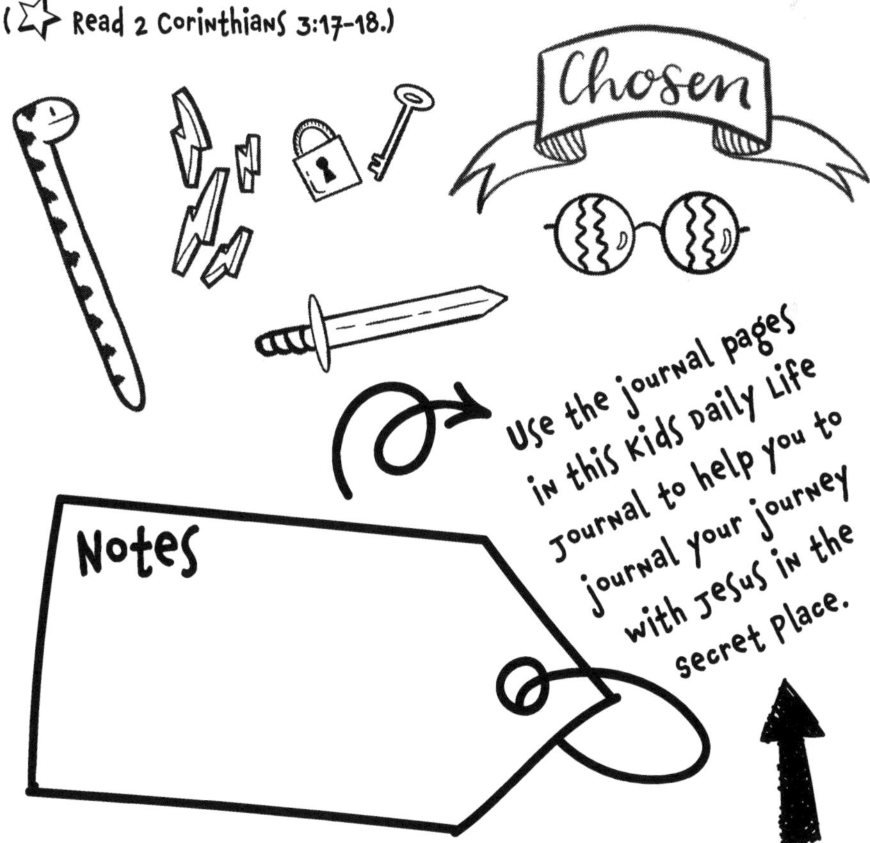

How to use your 2-YEAR DAILY READING & STUDY GUIDE

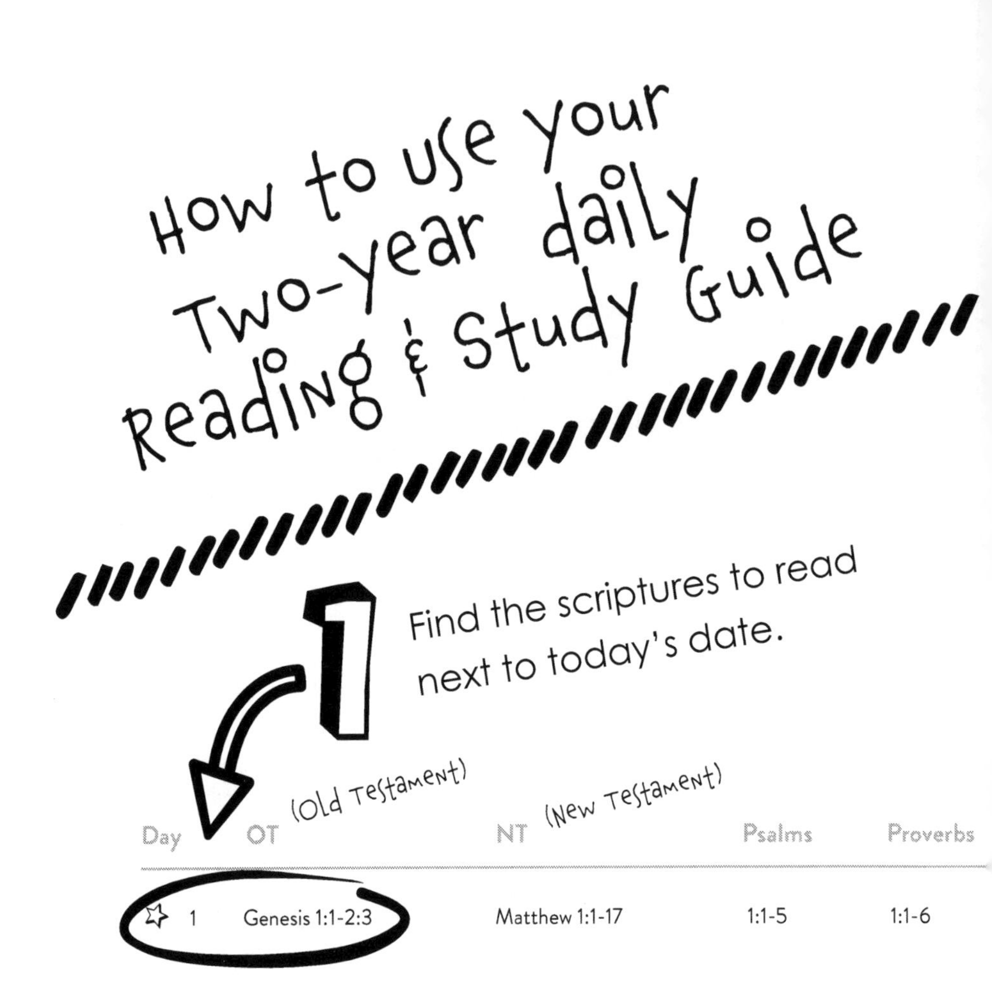

2 Look up the scriptures in your Bible.

3 As you read the scriptures, ask the Holy Spirit to help you to understand what the scriptures say, what they mean and what to do in obedience to them.

Talk with a parent, leader or friend in your life about what you read each day.

Using the journaling pages in your Kids Daily Life Journal, write out or draw pictures of what God is saying and showing you each day.

JANUARY

YEAR ONE

Day	OT	NT	Psalms	Proverbs
1	Genesis 1:1-2:3	Matthew 1:1-17	1:1-5	1:1-6
2	Genesis 2:4-25	Matthew 1:18-25	1:6	1:7-9
3	Genesis 3:1-24	Matthew 2:1-12	2:1-6	1:10-19
4	Genesis 4:1-26	Matthew 2:13-23	2:7-12	1:20-23
5	Genesis 5:1-32	Matthew 3:1-6	3:1-5	1:24-28
6	Genesis 6:1-22	Matthew 3:7-17	3:6-8	1:29-33
7	Genesis 7:1-24	Matthew 4:1-11	4:1-3	2:1-5
8	Genesis 8:1-9:19	Matthew 4:12-22	4:4-8	2:6-15
9	Genesis 9:20-10:32	Matthew 4:23-25	5:1-6	2:16-22
10	Genesis 11:1-26	Matthew 5:1-12	5:7-12	3:1-6
11	Genesis 11:27-13:4	Matthew 5:13-26	6:1-5	3:7-8
12	Genesis 13:5-14:16	Matthew 5:27-37	6:6-10	3:9-10
13	Genesis 14:17-15:21	Matthew 5:38-48	7:1-9	3:11-12
14	Genesis 16:1-17:14	Matthew 6:1-13	7:10-17	3:13-15
15	Genesis 17:15-18:15	Matthew 6:14-24	8:1	3:16-18
16	Genesis 18:16-19:26	Matthew 6:25-7:6	8:2-9	3:19-20
17	Genesis 19:27-38	Matthew 7:7-14	9:1-8	3:21-26
18	Genesis 20:1-21:21	Matthew 7:15-23	9:9-12	3:27-32
19	Genesis 21:22-22:24	Matthew 7:24-29	9:13-18	3:33-35
20	Genesis 23:1-20	Matthew 8:1-4	9:19-20	4:1-6
21	Genesis 24:1-51	Matthew 8:5-17	10:1-6	4:7-10
22	Genesis 24:52-25:28	Matthew 8:18-27	10:7-15	4:11-13
23	Genesis 25:29-26:16	Matthew 8:28-34	10:16	4:14-19
24	Genesis 26:17-35	Matthew 9:1-8	10:17-18	4:20-27
25	Genesis 27:1-45	Matthew 9:9-17	11:1-6	5:1-6
26	Genesis 27:46-28:22	Matthew 9:18-26	11:7	5:7-14
27	Genesis 29:1-35	Matthew 9:27-38	12:1-5	5:15-21
28	Genesis 30:1-24	Matthew 10:1-4	12:6-8	5:22-23
29	Genesis 30:25-31:16	Matthew 10:5-23	13:1-4	6:1-5
30	Genesis 31:17-55	Matthew 10:24-39	13:5-6	6:6-11
31	Genesis 32:1-12	Matthew 10:40-11:6	14:1-6	6:12-15

FEBRUARY

YEAR ONE

Day	OT	NT	Psalms	Proverbs
☆ 1	Genesis 32:13-33:20	Matthew 11:7-19	14:7	6:16-19
☆ 2	Genesis 34:1-31	Matthew 11:20-30	15:1-5	6:20-26
☆ 3	Genesis 35:1-36:8	Matthew 12:1-8	16:1-4	6:27-35
☆ 4	Genesis 36:9-43	Matthew 12:9-21	16:5-8	7:1-5
☆ 5	Genesis 37:1-36	Matthew 12:22-32	16:9-11	7:6-23
☆ 6	Genesis 38:1-30	Matthew 12:33-45	17:1-5	7:24-27
☆ 7	Genesis 39:1-23	Matthew 12:46-13:9	17:6-15	8:1-11
☆ 8	Genesis 40:1-41:16	Matthew 13:10-23	18:1-3	8:12-13
☆ 9	Genesis 41:17-52	Matthew 13:24-33	18:4-15	8:14-26
☆ 10	Genesis 41:53-42:17	Matthew 13:34-46	18:16-24	8:27-32
☆ 11	Genesis 42:18-38	Matthew 13:47-58	18:25-36	8:33-36
☆ 12	Genesis 43:1-34	Matthew 14:1-12	18:37-45	9:1-6
☆ 13	Genesis 44:1-45:15	Matthew 14:13-21	18:46-50	9:7-8
☆ 14	Genesis 45:16-46:7	Matthew 14:22-36	19:1-6	9:9-10
☆ 15	Genesis 46:8-47:12	Matthew 15:1-14	19:7-14	9:11-12
☆ 16	Genesis 47:13-31	Matthew 15:15-28	20:1-6	9:13-18
☆ 17	Genesis 48:1-22	Matthew 15:29-39	20:7-9	10:1-2
☆ 18	Genesis 49:1-33	Matthew 16:1-12	21:1-7	10:3-4
☆ 19	Genesis 50:1-26	Matthew 16:13-20	21:8-13	10:5
☆ 20	Exodus 1:1-2:10	Matthew 16:21-17:9	22:1-18	10:6-7
☆ 21	Exodus 2:11-22	Matthew 17:10-21	22:19-24	10:8-9
☆ 22	Exodus 2:23-3:22	Matthew 17:22-27	22:25-26	10:10
☆ 23	Exodus 4:1-26	Matthew 18:1-14	22:27-31	10:11-12
☆ 24	Exodus 4:27-5:21	Matthew 18:15-22	23:1-6	10:13-14
☆ 25	Exodus 5:22-6:30	Matthew 18:23-35	24:1-2	10:15-16
☆ 26	Exodus 7:1-25	Matthew 19:1-12	24:3-6	10:17
☆ 27	Exodus 8:1-32	Matthew 19:13-25	24:7-10	10:18
☆ 28*	Exodus 9:1-35	Matthew 19:26-30	25:1-7	10:19

** Note: When Leap Year occurs, divide the February 28 reading between February 28 and February 29.*

MARCH

YEAR ONE

Day	OT	NT	Psalms	Proverbs
☆ 1	Exodus 10:1-29	Matthew 20:1-16	25:8-15	10:20-21
☆ 2	Exodus 11:1-12:13	Matthew 20:17-28	25:16-22	10:22
☆ 3	Exodus 12:14-39	Matthew 20:29-21:11	26:1-8	10:23
☆ 4	Exodus 12:40-13:16	Matthew 21:12-22	26:9-12	10:24-25
☆ 5	Exodus 13:17-14:31	Matthew 21:23-32	27:1	10:26
☆ 6	Exodus 15:1-18	Matthew 21:33-46	27:2-3	10:27-28
☆ 7	Exodus 15:19-16:18	Matthew 22:1-22	27:4-6	10:29-30
☆ 8	Exodus 16:19-17:16	Matthew 22:23-33	27:7-10	10:31-32
☆ 9	Exodus 18:1-12	Matthew 22:34-46	27:11-14	11:1-3
☆ 10	Exodus 18:13-19:15	Matthew 23:1-12	28:1-5	11:4
☆ 11	Exodus 19:16-20:26	Matthew 23:13-26	28:6-9	11:5-6
☆ 12	Exodus 21:1-21	Matthew 23:27-39	29:1-2	11:7
☆ 13	Exodus 21:22-22:13	Matthew 24:1-14	29:3-11	11:8
☆ 14	Exodus 22:14-23:13	Matthew 24:15-28	30:1-3	11:9-11
☆ 15	Exodus 23:14-24:2	Matthew 24:29-36	30:4-12	11:12-13
☆ 16	Exodus 24:3-25:30	Matthew 24:37-51	31:1-2	11:14
☆ 17	Exodus 25:31-26:29	Matthew 25:1-13	31:3-8	11:15
☆ 18	Exodus 26:30-27:21	Matthew 25:14-30	31:9-18	11:16-17
☆ 19	Exodus 28:1-14	Matthew 25:31-46	31:19-20	11:18-19
☆ 20	Exodus 28:15-43	Matthew 26:1-13	31:21-22	11:20-21
☆ 21	Exodus 29:1-28	Matthew 26:14-25	31:23-24	11:22
☆ 22	Exodus 29:29-30:10	Matthew 26:26-46	32:1-7	11:23
☆ 23	Exodus 30:11-38	Matthew 26:47-56	32:8-11	11:24-26
☆ 24	Exodus 31:1-18	Matthew 26:57-68	33:1-5	11:27
☆ 25	Exodus 32:1-30	Matthew 26:69-75	33:6-11	11:28
☆ 26	Exodus 32:31-33:23	Matthew 27:1-14	33:12-19	11:29-31
☆ 27	Exodus 34:1-14	Matthew 27:15-26	33:20-22	12:1
☆ 28	Exodus 34:15-35:9	Matthew 27:27-31	34:1-3	12:2-3
☆ 29	Exodus 35:10-36:7	Matthew 27:32-53	34:4-10	12:4
☆ 30	Exodus 36:8-38	Matthew 27:54-66	34:11-14	12:5-7
☆ 31	Exodus 37:1-38:8	Matthew 28:1-10	34:15-22	12:8-9

APRIL

YEAR ONE

Day	OT	NT	Psalms	Proverbs
☆ 1	Exodus 38:9-31	Matthew 28:11-20	35:1-9	12:10
☆ 2	Exodus 39:1-43	Mark 1:1-15	35:10-18	12:11
☆ 3	Exodus 40:1-38	Mark 1:16-28	35:19-28	12:12-14
☆ 4	Leviticus 1:1-17	Mark 1:29-45	36:1-5	12:15-17
☆ 5	Leviticus 2:1-3:17	Mark 2:1-12	36:6-9	12:18
☆ 6	Leviticus 4:1-26	Mark 2:13-22	36:10-12	12:19-20
☆ 7	Leviticus 4:27-5:19	Mark 2:23-3:6	37:1-6	12:21-23
☆ 8	Leviticus 6:1-23	Mark 3:7-19	37:7-11	12:24
☆ 9	Leviticus 6:24-7:27	Mark 3:20-30	37:12-20	12:25
☆ 10	Leviticus 7:28-8:17	Mark 3:31-4:9	37:21-29	12:26
☆ 11	Leviticus 8:18-9:6	Mark 4:10-25	37:30-33	12:27-28
☆ 12	Leviticus 9:7-24	Mark 4:26-41	37:34-40	13:1
☆ 13	Leviticus 10:1-20	Mark 5:1-20	38:1-18	13:2-3
☆ 14	Leviticus 11:1-47	Mark 5:21-34	38:19-22	13:4
☆ 15	Leviticus 12:1-8	Mark 5:35-43	39:1-5	13:5-6
☆ 16	Leviticus 13:1-23	Mark 6:1-15	39:6-13	13:7-8
☆ 17	Leviticus 13:24-59	Mark 6:16-29	40:1-3	13:9-10
☆ 18	Leviticus 14:1-32	Mark 6:30-44	40:4-10	13:11
☆ 19	Leviticus 14:33-57	Mark 6:45-56	40:11-13	13:12-14
☆ 20	Leviticus 15:1-33	Mark 7:1-8	40:14-17	13:15-16
☆ 21	Leviticus 16:1-28	Mark 7:9-23	41:1-3	13:17-19
☆ 22	Leviticus 16:29-17:16	Mark 7:24-8:10	41:4-13	13:20-23
☆ 23	Leviticus 18:1-30	Mark 8:11-26	42:1-8	13:24-25
☆ 24	Leviticus 19:1-34	Mark 8:27-38	42:9-11	14:1-2
☆ 25	Leviticus 19:35-20:21	Mark 9:1-13	43:1-4	14:3-4
☆ 26	Leviticus 20:22-21:24	Mark 9:14-29	43:5	14:5-6
☆ 27	Leviticus 22:1-16	Mark 9:30-37	44:1-3	14:7-8
☆ 28	Leviticus 22:17-23:21	Mark 9:38-50	44:4-8	14:9-10
☆ 29	Leviticus 23:22-44	Mark 10:1-12	44:9-22	14:11-12
☆ 30	Leviticus 24:1-25:13	Mark 10:13-16	44:23-26	14:13-14

MAY

YEAR ONE

Day	OT	NT	Psalms	Proverbs
☆ 1	Leviticus 25:14-46	Mark 10:17-31	45:1-6	14:15-16
☆ 2	Leviticus 25:47-26:13	Mark 10:32-45	45:7-17	14:17-19
☆ 3	Leviticus 26:14-46	Mark 10:46-52	46:1-7	14:20-21
☆ 4	Leviticus 27:1-34	Mark 11:1-11	46:8-11	14:22-24
☆ 5	Numbers 1:1-54	Mark 11:12-25	47:1-7	14:25
☆ 6	Numbers 2:1-3:10	Mark 11:27-33	47:8-9	14:26-27
☆ 7	Numbers 3:11-51	Mark 12:1-17	48:1-8	14:28-29
☆ 8	Numbers 4:1-49	Mark 12:18-34	48:9-14	14:30-31
☆ 9	Numbers 5:1-31	Mark 12:35-37	49:1-9	14:32-33
☆ 10	Numbers 6:1-7:9	Mark 12:38-44	49:10-20	14:34-35
☆ 11	Numbers 7:10-89	Mark 13:1-13	50:1-6	15:1-3
☆ 12	Numbers 8:1-9:3	Mark 13:14-27	50:7-23	15:4
☆ 13	Numbers 9:4-23	Mark 13:28-37	51:1-9	15:5-7
☆ 14	Numbers 10:1-36	Mark 14:1-11	51:10-19	15:8-10
☆ 15	Numbers 11:1-23	Mark 14:12-21	52:1-7	15:11
☆ 16	Numbers 11:24-12:16	Mark 14:22-31	52:8-9	15:12-14
☆ 17	Numbers 13:1-33	Mark 14:32-52	53:1-5	15:15-17
☆ 18	Numbers 14:1-25	Mark 14:53-65	53:6	15:18-19
☆ 19	Numbers 14:26-15:16	Mark 14:66-72	54:1-4	15:20-21
☆ 20	Numbers 15:17-41	Mark 15:1-24	54:5-7	15:22-23
☆ 21	Numbers 16:1-40	Mark 15:25-32	55:1-11	15:24-26
☆ 22	Numbers 16:41-18:7	Mark 15:33-47	55:12-23	15:27-28
☆ 23	Numbers 18:8-32	Mark 16:1-8	56:1-9	15:29-30
☆ 24	Numbers 19:1-22	Mark 16:9-20	56:10-13	15:31-32
☆ 25	Numbers 20:1-29	Luke 1:1-7	57:1-3	15:33
☆ 26	Numbers 21:1-30	Luke 1:8-25	57:4-11	16:1-3
☆ 27	Numbers 21:31-22:20	Luke 1:26-38	58:1-9	16:4-5
☆ 28	Numbers 22:21-41	Luke 1:39-56	58:10-11	16:6-7
☆ 29	Numbers 23:1-30	Luke 1:57-66	59:1-13	16:8-9
☆ 30	Numbers 24:1-25	Luke 1:67-80	59:14-17	16:10-11
☆ 31	Numbers 25:1-18	Luke 2:1-20	60:1-5	16:12-13

JUNE

YEAR ONE

Day	OT	NT	Psalms	Proverbs
☆ 1	Numbers 26:1-37	Luke 2:21-35	60:6-12	16:14-15
☆ 2	Numbers 26:38-51	Luke 2:36-40	61:1-3	16:16-17
☆ 3	Numbers 26:52-27:11	Luke 2:41-52	61:4-8	16:18
☆ 4	Numbers 27:12-28:15	Luke 3:1-14	62:1-8	16:19-20
☆ 5	Numbers 28:16-29:11	Luke 3:15-22	62:9-12	16:21-23
☆ 6	Numbers 29:12-40	Luke 3:23-28	63:1-5	16:24
☆ 7	Numbers 30:1-31:24	Luke 3:29-4:13	63:6-11	16:25
☆ 8	Numbers 31:25-54	Luke 4:14-30	64:1-9	16:26-27
☆ 9	Numbers 32:1-42	Luke 4:31-44	64:10	16:28-30
☆ 10	Numbers 33:1-39	Luke 5:1-11	65:1-4	16:31-33
☆ 11	Numbers 33:40-34:29	Luke 5:12-16	65:5-13	17:1
☆ 12	Numbers 35:1-34	Luke 5:17-28	66:1-7	17:2-3
☆ 13	Numbers 36:1-13	Luke 5:29-39	66:8-20	17:4-5
☆ 14	Deuteronomy 1:1-46	Luke 6:1-11	67:1-3	17:6
☆ 15	Deuteronomy 2:1-37	Luke 6:12-19	67:4-7	17:7-8
☆ 16	Deuteronomy 3:1-29	Luke 6:20-38	68:1-6	17:9-11
☆ 17	Deuteronomy 4:1-20	Luke 6:39-49	68:7-18	17:12-13
☆ 18	Deuteronomy 4:21-49	Luke 7:1-10	68:19-31	17:14-15
☆ 19	Deuteronomy 5:1-31	Luke 7:11-23	68:32-35	17:16
☆ 20	Deuteronomy 5:32-6:25	Luke 7:24-35	69:1-13	17:17-18
☆ 21	Deuteronomy 7:1-26	Luke 7:36-50	69:14-18	17:19-21
☆ 22	Deuteronomy 8:1-20	Luke 8:1-3	69:19-31	17:22
☆ 23	Deuteronomy 9:1-10:5	Luke 8:4-15	69:32-36	17:23
☆ 24	Deuteronomy 10:6-22	Luke 8:16-21	70:1-5	17:24-25
☆ 25	Deuteronomy 11:1-32	Luke 8:22-25	71:1-6	17:26
☆ 26	Deuteronomy 12:1-32	Luke 8:26-39	71:7-16	17:27-28
☆ 27	Deuteronomy 13:1-14:27	Luke 8:40-56	71:17-24	18:1
☆ 28	Deuteronomy 14:28-15:23	Luke 9:1-6	72:1-14	18:2-3
☆ 29	Deuteronomy 16:1-22	Luke 9:7-17	72:15-20	18:4-5
☆ 30	Deuteronomy 17:1-20	Luke 9:18-27	73:1-20	18:6-7

JULY

YEAR ONE

Day	OT	NT	Psalms	Proverbs
☆ 1	Deuteronomy 18:1-19:14	Luke 9:28-36	73:21-28	18:8
☆ 2	Deuteronomy 19:15-20:20	Luke 9:37-50	74:1-11	18:9-10
☆ 3	Deuteronomy 21:1-23	Luke 9:51-62	74:12-23	18:11-12
☆ 4	Deuteronomy 22:1-30	Luke 10:1-12	75:1-5	18:13
☆ 5	Deuteronomy 23:1-24:13	Luke 10:13-24	75:6-10	18:14-15
☆ 6	Deuteronomy 24:14-25:19	Luke 10:25-37	76:1-7	18:16-18
☆ 7	Deuteronomy 26:1-19	Luke 10:38-42	76:8-12	18:19
☆ 8	Deuteronomy 27:1-26	Luke 11:1-13	77:1-14	18:20-21
☆ 9	Deuteronomy 28:1-44	Luke 11:14-22	77:15-20	18:22
☆ 10	Deuteronomy 28:45-68	Luke 11:23-36	78:1-22	18:23-24
☆ 11	Deuteronomy 29:1-29	Luke 11:37-54	78:23-31	19:1-3
☆ 12	Deuteronomy 30:1-20	Luke 12:1-7	78:32-39	19:4-5
☆ 13	Deuteronomy 31:1-29	Luke 12:8-12	78:40-55	19:6-7
☆ 14	Deuteronomy 31:30-32:27	Luke 12:13-34	78:56-59	19:8-9
☆ 15	Deuteronomy 32:28-52	Luke 12:35-48	78:60-64	19:10-12
☆ 16	Deuteronomy 33:1-17	Luke 12:49-59	78:65-69	19:13-14
☆ 17	Deuteronomy 33:18-29	Luke 13:1-9	78:70-72	19:15-16
☆ 18	Deuteronomy 34:1-Joshua 1:18	Luke 13:10-21	79:1-8	19:17
☆ 19	Joshua 2:1-24	Luke 13:22-35	79:9-13	19:18-19
☆ 20	Joshua 3:1-17	Luke 14:1-6	80:1-13	19:20-21
☆ 21	Joshua 4:1-24	Luke 14:7-24	80:14-19	19:22-23
☆ 22	Joshua 5:1-15	Luke 14:25-35	81:1-7	19:24-25
☆ 23	Joshua 6:1-27	Luke 15:1-10	81:8-16	19:26
☆ 24	Joshua 7:1-26	Luke 15:11-32	82:1-5	19:27-29
☆ 25	Joshua 8:1-9:2	Luke 16:1-9	82:6-8	20:1
☆ 26	Joshua 9:3-10:11	Luke 16:10-18	83:1-8	20:2-3
☆ 27	Joshua 10:12-43	Luke 16:19-31	83:9-18	20:4-6
☆ 28	Joshua 11:1-23	Luke 17:1-10	84:1-4	20:7
☆ 29	Joshua 12:1-24	Luke 17:11-25	84:5-12	20:8-10
☆ 30	Joshua 13:1-33	Luke 17:26-37	85:1-7	20:11
31	Joshua 14:1-15	Luke 18:1-8	85:8-13	20:12

AUGUST

YEAR ONE

Day	OT	NT	Psalms	Proverbs
☆ 1	Joshua 15:1-12	Luke 18:9-17	86:1-7	20:13-15
☆ 2	Joshua 15:13-63	Luke 18:18-30	86:8-17	20:16-18
☆ 3	Joshua 16:1-17:18	Luke 18:31-43	87:1-3	20:19
☆ 4	Joshua 18:1-28	Luke 19:1-10	87:4-7	20:20-21
☆ 5	Joshua 19:1-31	Luke 19:11-27	88:1-12	20:22-23
☆ 6	Joshua 19:32-20:9	Luke 19:28-40	88:13-18	20:24-25
☆ 7	Joshua 21:1-42	Luke 19:41-48	89:1-6	20:26-27
☆ 8	Joshua 21:43-22:20	Luke 20:1-8	89:7-13	20:28-30
☆ 9	Joshua 22:21-34	Luke 20:9-26	89:14-18	21:1-2
☆ 10	Joshua 23:1-16	Luke 20:27-40	89:19-37	21:3
☆ 11	Joshua 24:1-28	Luke 20:41-47	89:38-45	21:4
☆ 12	Joshua 24:29-Judges 1:15	Luke 21:1-4	89:46-52	21:5-7
☆ 13	Judges 1:16-36	Luke 21:5-28	90:1-17	21:8-10
☆ 14	Judges 2:1-9	Luke 21:29-36	91:1-16	21:11-12
☆ 15	Judges 2:10-23	Luke 21:37-22:13	92:1-15	21:13
☆ 16	Judges 3:1-31	Luke 22:14-23	93:1-5	21:14-16
☆ 17	Judges 4:1-24	Luke 22:24-34	94:1-13	21:17-18
☆ 18	Judges 5:1-31	Luke 22:35-38	94:14-23	21:19-20
☆ 19	Judges 6:1-32	Luke 22:39-53	95:1-11	21:21-22
☆ 20	Judges 6:33-40	Luke 22:54-71	96:1-13	21:23-24
☆ 21	Judges 7:1-25	Luke 23:1-12	97:1-12	21:25-26
☆ 22	Judges 8:1-17	Luke 23:13-25	98:1-9	21:27
☆ 23	Judges 8:18-32	Luke 23:26-43	99:1-4	21:28-29
☆ 24	Judges 8:33-9:21	Luke 23:44-56	99:5-9	21:30-31
☆ 25	Judges 9:22-57	Luke 24:1-12	100:1-2	22:1
☆ 26	Judges 10:1-18	Luke 24:13-34	100:3-5	22:2-4
☆ 27	Judges 11:1-28	Luke 24:35-53	101:1-3	22:5-6
☆ 28	Judges 11:29-12:15	John 1:1-18	101:4-8	22:7
☆ 29	Judges 13:1-25	John 1:19-28	102:1-17	22:8-9
☆ 30	Judges 14:1-20	John 1:29-42	102:18-22	22:10-12
☆ 31	Judges 15:1-16:9	John 1:43-51	102:23-28	22:13

SEPTEMBER

YEAR ONE

Day	OT	NT	Psalms	Proverbs
☆ 1	Judges 16:10-31	John 2:1-11	103:1-12	22:14
☆ 2	Judges 17:1-18:21	John 2:12-25	103:13-22	22:15
☆ 3	Judges 18:22-31	John 3:1-15	104:1-7	22:16
☆ 4	Judges 19:1-30	John 3:16-21	104:8-23	22:17-19
☆ 5	Judges 20:1-48	John 3:22-30	104:24-30	22:20-21
☆ 6	Judges 21:1-25	John 3:31-4:3	104:31-35	22:22-23
☆ 7	Ruth 1:1-22	John 4:4-30	105:1-7	22:24-25
☆ 8	Ruth 2:1-3:6	John 4:31-42	105:8-15	22:26-27
☆ 9	Ruth 3:7-4:22	John 4:43-45	105:16-26	22:28-29
☆ 10	1 Samuel 1:1-23	John 4:46-54	105:27-36	23:1-3
☆ 11	1 Samuel 1:24-2:21	John 5:1-18	105:37-45	23:4-5
☆ 12	1 Samuel 2:22-3:18	John 5:19-23	106:1-2	23:6-8
☆ 13	1 Samuel 3:19-4:22	John 5:24-38	106:3-5	23:9-11
☆ 14	1 Samuel 5:1-6:12	John 5:39-47	106:6-12	23:12
☆ 15	1 Samuel 6:13-7:17	John 6:1-15	106:13-23	23:13-14
☆ 16	1 Samuel 8:1-22	John 6:16-21	106:24-31	23:15-16
☆ 17	1 Samuel 9:1-27	John 6:22-29	106:32-46	23:17-18
☆ 18	1 Samuel 10:1-27	John 6:30-42	106:47-48	23:19-21
☆ 19	1 Samuel 11:1-15	John 6:43-52	107:1-3	23:22
☆ 20	1 Samuel 12:1-25	John 6:53-71	107:4-32	23:23
☆ 21	1 Samuel 13:1-23	John 7:1-13	107:33-43	23:24
☆ 22	1 Samuel 14:1-23	John 7:14-30	108:1-4	23:25-28
☆ 23	1 Samuel 14:24-52	John 7:31-36	108:5-13	23:29-35
☆ 24	1 Samuel 15:1-35	John 7:37-53	109:1-21	24:1-2
☆ 25	1 Samuel 16:1-23	John 8:1-11	109:22-31	24:3-4
☆ 26	1 Samuel 17:1-40	John 8:12-20	110:1-3	24:5-6
☆ 27	1 Samuel 17:41-18:4	John 8:21-24	110:4-7	24:7
☆ 28	1 Samuel 18:5:30	John 8:25-30	111:1-4	24:8
☆ 29	1 Samuel 19:1-24	John 8:31-36	111:5-10	24:9-10
☆ 30	1 Samuel 20:1-34	John 8:37-59	112:1-3	24:11-12

OCTOBER

YEAR ONE

Day	OT	NT	Psalms	Proverbs
☆ 1	1 Samuel 20:35-21:15	John 9:1-13	112:4-10	24:13-14
☆ 2	1 Samuel 22:1-23	John 9:14-41	113:1-9	24:15-16
☆ 3	1 Samuel 23:1-29	John 10:1-10	114:1-8	24:17-20
☆ 4	1 Samuel 24:1-22	John 10:11-21	115:1-10	24:21-22
☆ 5	1 Samuel 25:1-44	John 10:22-29	115:11-18	24:23-25
☆ 6	1 Samuel 26:1-25	John 10:30-42	116:1-5	24:26
☆ 7	1 Samuel 27:1-28:25	John 11:1-29	116:6-14	24:27
☆ 8	1 Samuel 29:1-30:20	John 11:30-54	116:15-117:2	24:28-29
☆ 9	1 Samuel 30:21-31:13	John 11:55-12:8	118:1-7	24:30-34
☆ 10	2 Samuel 1:1-16	John 12:9-19	118:8-18	25:1-5
☆ 11	2 Samuel 1:17-2:11	John 12:20-36	118:19-26	25:6-8
☆ 12	2 Samuel 2:12-3:5	John 12:37-50	118:27-29	25:9-10
☆ 13	2 Samuel 3:6-39	John 13:1-20	119:1-8	25:11-14
☆ 14	2 Samuel 4:1-5:12	John 13:21-30	119:9-16	25:15
☆ 15	2 Samuel 5:13-6:23	John 13:31-38	119:17-24	25:16
☆ 16	2 Samuel 7:1-29	John 14:1-14	119:25-32	25:17
☆ 17	2 Samuel 8:1-18	John 14:15-26	119:33-40	25:18-19
☆ 18	2 Samuel 9:1-10:19	John 14:27-31	119:41-48	25:20-22
☆ 19	2 Samuel 11:1-27	John 15:1-17	119:49-58	25:23-24
☆ 20	2 Samuel 12:1-14	John 15:18-27	119:59-64	25:25-27
☆ 21	2 Samuel 12:15-31	John 16:1-16	119:65-72	25:28
☆ 22	2 Samuel 13:1-22	John 16:17-33	119:73-80	26:1-2
☆ 23	2 Samuel 13:23-39	John 17:1-26	119:81-88	26:3-5
☆ 24	2 Samuel 14:1-33	John 18:1-14	119:89-96	26:6-8
☆ 25	2 Samuel 15:1-22	John 18:15-24	119:97-104	26:9-12
☆ 26	2 Samuel 15:23-16:4	John 18:25-19:22	119:105-112	26:13-16
☆ 27	2 Samuel 16:5-23	John 19:23-30	119:113-120	26:17
☆ 28	2 Samuel 17:1-16	John 19:31-42	119:121-128	26:18-19
☆ 29	2 Samuel 17:17-29	John 20:1-18	119:129-136	26:20
☆ 30	2 Samuel 18:1-18	John 20:19-31	119:137-152	26:21-22
☆ 31	2 Samuel 18:19-19:10	John 21:1-14	119:153-159	26:23

NOVEMBER

YEAR ONE

Day	OT	NT	Psalms	Proverbs
1	2 Samuel 19:11-40	John 21:15-25	119:160-168	26:24-26
2	2 Samuel 19:41-20:13	Acts 1:1-14	119:169-176	26:27
3	2 Samuel 20:14-26	Acts 1:15-26	120:1-7	26:28
4	2 Samuel 21:1-22	Acts 2:1-21	121:1-4	27:1-2
5	2 Samuel 22:1-46	Acts 2:22-47	121:5-8	27:3
6	2 Samuel 22:47-23:23	Acts 3:1-11	122:1-5	27:4-6
7	2 Samuel 23:24-24:9	Acts 3:12-26	122:6-9	27:7-9
8	2 Samuel 24:10-25	Acts 4:1-22	123:1-2	27:10
9	1 Kings 1:1-37	Acts 4:23-37	123:3-4	27:11
10	1 Kings 1:38-53	Acts 5:1-11	124:1-6	27:12
11	1 Kings 2:1-25	Acts 5:12-42	124:7-8	27:13
12	1 Kings 2:26-3:2	Acts 6:1-6	125:1-3	27:14
13	1 Kings 3:3-28	Acts 6:7-15	125:4-5	27:15-16
14	1 Kings 4:1-34	Acts 7:1-10	126:1-3	27:17
15	1 Kings 5:1-6:13	Acts 7:11-29	126:4-6	27:18-20
16	1 Kings 6:14-38	Acts 7:30-43	127:1-2	27:21-22
17	1 Kings 7:1-26	Acts 7:44-50	127:3-5	27:23-27
18	1 Kings 7:27-51	Acts 7:51-60	128:1-4	28:1
19	1 Kings 8:1-21	Acts 8:1-13	128:5-6	28:2
20	1 Kings 8:22-66	Acts 8:14-24	129:1-4	28:3-5
21	1 Kings 9:1-28	Acts 8:25-40	129:5-8	28:6-7
22	1 Kings 10:1-29	Acts 9:1-9	130:1-5	28:8-10
23	1 Kings 11:1-28	Acts 9:10-25	130:6-8	28:11
24	1 Kings 11:29-12:19	Acts 9:26-35	131:1-132:9	28:12-13
25	1 Kings 12:20-13:6	Acts 9:36-43	132:10-12	28:14
26	1 Kings 13:7-34	Acts 10:1-8	132:13-18	28:15-16
27	1 Kings 14:1-31	Acts 10:9-23	133:1-2	28:17-18
28	1 Kings 15:1-24	Acts 10:24-33	133:3	28:19-20
29	1 Kings 15:25-16:28	Acts 10:34-48	134:1-135:4	28:21-22
30	1 Kings 16:29-17:24	Acts 11:1-18	135:5-12	28:23-24

DECEMBER

YEAR ONE

Day	OT	NT	Psalms	Proverbs
1	1 Kings 18:1-19	Acts 11:19-30	135:13-21	28:25-26
2	1 Kings 18:20-46	Acts 12:1-19	136:1-12	28:27-28
3	1 Kings 19:1-14	Acts 12:20-23	136:13-26	29:1
4	1 Kings 19:15-20:15	Acts 12:24-13:12	137:1-4	29:2-4
5	1 Kings 20:16-43	Acts 13:13-15	137:5-9	29:5-8
6	1 Kings 21:1-29	Acts 13:16-25	138:1-6	29:9-11
7	1 Kings 22:1-28	Acts 13:26-37	138:7-8	29:12-14
8	1 Kings 22:29-53	Acts 13:38-43	139:1-12	29:15-17
9	2 Kings 1:1-18	Acts 13:44-14:7	139:13-24	29:18
10	2 Kings 2:1-25	Acts 14:8-20	140:1-8	29:19-20
11	2 Kings 3:1-27	Acts 14:21-28	140:9-13	29:21-22
12	2 Kings 4:1-17	Acts 15:1-21	141:1-2	29:23
13	2 Kings 4:18-44	Acts 15:22-35	141:3-10	29:24-25
14	2 Kings 5:1-27	Acts 15:36-16:5	142:1-3	29:26-27
15	2 Kings 6:1-23	Acts 16:6-15	142:4-7	30:1-4
16	2 Kings 6:24-7:20	Acts 16:16-24	143:1-6	30:5-6
17	2 Kings 8:1-19	Acts 16:25-40	143:7-12	30:7-9
18	2 Kings 8:20-9:13	Acts 17:1-9	144:1-8	30:10
19	2 Kings 9:14-37	Acts 17:10-15	144:9-15	30:11-14
20	2 Kings 10:1-31	Acts 17:16-34	145:1-7	30:15-16
21	2 Kings 10:32-11:20	Acts 18:1-11	145:8-21	30:17
22	2 Kings 11:21-12:21	Acts 18:12-22	146:1-2	30:18-20
23	2 Kings 13:1-25	Acts 18:23-28	146:3-10	30:21-23
24	2 Kings 14:1-29	Acts 19:1-12	147:1-11	30:24-28
25	2 Kings 15:1-31	Acts 19:13-22	147:12-20	30:29-31
26	2 Kings 15:32-16:20	Acts 19:23-41	148:1-4	30:32
27	2 Kings 17:1-28	Acts 20:1-15	148:5-14	30:33
28	2 Kings 17:29-18:12	Acts 20:16-38	149:1	31:1-7
29	2 Kings 18:13-19:4	Acts 21:1-6	149:2-9	31:8-9
30	2 Kings 19:5-37	Acts 21:7-17	150:1-5	31:10-24
31	2 Kings 20:1-21	Acts 21:18-26	150:6	31:25-31

JANUARY

YEAR TWO

Day	OT	NT	Psalms	Proverbs
☆ 1	2 Kings 21:1-22:2	Acts 21:27-36	1:1-5	1:1-6
☆ 2	2 Kings 22:3-23:7	Acts 21:37-40	1:6	1:7-9
☆ 3	2 Kings 23:8-30	Acts 22:1-16	2:1-6	1:10-19
☆ 4	2 Kings 23:31-25:7	Acts 22:17-30	2:7-12	1:20-23
☆ 5	2 Kings 25:8-30	Acts 23:1-10	3:1-5	1:24-28
☆ 6	1 Chronicles 1:1-33	Acts 23:11-15	3:6-8	1:29-33
☆ 7	1 Chronicles 1:34-2:17	Acts 23:16-35	4:1-3	2:1-5
☆ 8	1 Chronicles 2:18-55	Acts 24:1-23	4:4-8	2:6-15
☆ 9	1 Chronicles 3:1-4:4	Acts 24:24-27	5:1-6	2:16-22
☆ 10	1 Chronicles 4:5-37	Acts 25:1-13	5:7-12	3:1-6
☆ 11	1 Chronicles 4:38-5:17	Acts 25:14-27	6:1-5	3:7-8
☆ 12	1 Chronicles 5:18-6:30	Acts 26:1-8	6:6-10	3:9-10
☆ 13	1 Chronicles 6:31-81	Acts 26:9-32	7:1-9	3:11-12
☆ 14	1 Chronicles 7:1-40	Acts 27:1-6	7:10-17	3:13-15
☆ 15	1 Chronicles 8:1-40	Acts 27:7-20	8:1	3:16-18
☆ 16	1 Chronicles 9:1-16	Acts 27:21-32	8:2-9	3:19-20
☆ 17	1 Chronicles 9:17-10:14	Acts 27:33-44	9:1-8	3:21-26
☆ 18	1 Chronicles 11:1-25	Acts 28:1-16	9:9-12	3:27-32
☆ 19	1 Chronicles 11:26-12:18	Acts 28:17-31	9:13-18	3:33-35
☆ 20	1 Chronicles 12:19-40	Romans 1:1-9	9:19-20	4:1-6
☆ 21	1 Chronicles 13:1-14:17	Romans 1:10-17	10:1-6	4:7-10
☆ 22	1 Chronicles 15:1-29	Romans 1:18-20	10:7-15	4:11-13
☆ 23	1 Chronicles 16:1-36	Romans 1:21-32	10:16	4:14-19
☆ 24	1 Chronicles 16:37-17:15	Romans 2:1-11	10:17-18	4:20-27
☆ 25	1 Chronicles 17:16-18:17	Romans 2:12-24	11:1-6	5:1-6
☆ 26	1 Chronicles 19:1-20:8	Romans 2:25-29	11:7	5:7-14
☆ 27	1 Chronicles 21:1-30	Romans 3:1-8	12:1-5	5:15-21
☆ 28	1 Chronicles 22:1-19	Romans 3:9-22	12:6-8	5:22-23
☆ 29	1 Chronicles 23:1-32	Romans 3:23-31	13:1-4	6:1-5
☆ 30	1 Chronicles 24:1-31	Romans 4:1-10	13:5-6	6:6-11
☆ 31	1 Chronicles 25:1-26:11	Romans 4:11-12	14:1-6	6:12-15

FEBRUARY

YEAR TWO

Day	OT	NT	Psalms	Proverbs
☆ 1	1 Chronicles 26:12-32	Romans 4:13-17	14:7	6:16-19
☆ 2	1 Chronicles 27:1-34	Romans 4:18-5:5	15:1-5	6:20-26
☆ 3	1 Chronicles 28:1-21	Romans 5:6-11	16:1-4	6:27-35
☆ 4	1 Chronicles 29:1-30	Romans 5:12-21	16:5-8	7:1-5
☆ 5	2 Chronicles 1:1-2:10	Romans 6:1-14	16:9-11	7:6-23
☆ 6	2 Chronicles 2:11-3:17	Romans 6:15-23	17:1-5	7:24-27
☆ 7	2 Chronicles 4:1-22	Romans 7:1-4	17:6-15	8:1-11
☆ 8	2 Chronicles 5:1-6:11	Romans 7:5-13	18:1-3	8:12-13
☆ 9	2 Chronicles 6:12-42	Romans 7:14-25	18:4-15	8:14-26
☆ 10	2 Chronicles 7:1-8:10	Romans 8:1-8	18:16-24	8:27-32
☆ 11	2 Chronicles 8:11-9:12	Romans 8:9-11	18:25-36	8:33-36
☆ 12	2 Chronicles 9:13-10:19	Romans 8:12-25	18:37-45	9:1-6
☆ 13	2 Chronicles 11:1-12:16	Romans 8:26-34	18:46-50	9:7-8
☆ 14	2 Chronicles 13:1-22	Romans 8:35-39	19:1-6	9:9-10
☆ 15	2 Chronicles 14:1-15:8	Romans 9:1-10	19:7-14	9:11-12
☆ 16	2 Chronicles 15:9-16:14	Romans 9:11-24	20:1-6	9:13-18
☆ 17	2 Chronicles 17:1-19	Romans 9:25-33	20:7-9	10:1-2
☆ 18	2 Chronicles 18:1-34	Romans 10:1-13	21:1-7	10:3-4
☆ 19	2 Chronicles 19:1-11	Romans 10:14-21	21:8-13	10:5
☆ 20	2 Chronicles 20:1-37	Romans 11:1-12	22:1-18	10:6-7
☆ 21	2 Chronicles 21:1-20	Romans 11:13-21	22:19-24	10:8-9
☆ 22	2 Chronicles 22:1-23:21	Romans 11:22-36	22:25-26	10:10
☆ 23	2 Chronicles 24:1-27	Romans 12:1-8	22:27-31	10:11-12
☆ 24	2 Chronicles 25:1-28	Romans 12:9-21	23:1-6	10:13-14
☆ 25	2 Chronicles 26:1-27:9	Romans 13:1-7	24:1-2	10:15-16
☆ 26	2 Chronicles 28:1-27	Romans 13:8-14	24:3-6	10:17
☆ 27	2 Chronicles 29:1-17	Romans 14:1-9	24:7-10	10:18
☆ 28*	2 Chronicles 29:18-36	Romans 14:10-15:4	25:1-7	10:19

** Note: When Leap Year occurs, divide the February 28 reading between February 28 and February 29.*

MARCH

YEAR TWO

Day	OT	NT	Psalms	Proverbs
1	2 Chronicles 30:1-20	Romans 15:5-13	25:8-15	10:20-21
2	2 Chronicles 30:21-31:21	Romans 15:14-22	25:16-22	10:22
3	2 Chronicles 32:1-23	Romans 15:23-33	26:1-8	10:23
4	2 Chronicles 32:24-33:13	Romans 16:1-9	26:9-12	10:24-25
5	2 Chronicles 33:14-34:13	Romans 16:10-20	27:1	10:26
6	2 Chronicles 34:14-33	Romans 16:21-27	27:2-3	10:27-28
7	2 Chronicles 35:1-27	1 Cor 1:1-9	27:4-6	10:29-30
8	2 Chronicles 36:1-23	1 Cor 1:10-17	27:7-10	10:31-32
9	Ezra 1:1-2:35	1 Cor 1:18-25	27:11-14	11:1-3
10	Ezra 2:36-70	1 Cor 1:26-2:5	28:1-5	11:4
11	Ezra 3:1-13	1 Cor 2:6-16	28:6-9	11:5-6
12	Ezra 4:1-24	1 Cor 3:1-4	29:1-2	11:7
13	Ezra 5:1-6:1	1 Cor 3:5-15	29:3-11	11:8
14	Ezra 6:2-22	1 Cor 3:16-23	30:1-3	11:9-11
15	Ezra 7:1-26	1 Cor 4:1-9	30:4-12	11:12-13
16	Ezra 7:27-8:20	1 Cor 4:10-21	31:1-2	11:14
17	Ezra 8:21-36	1 Cor 5:1-8	31:3-8	11:15
18	Ezra 9:1-15	1 Cor 5:9-13	31:9-18	11:16-17
19	Ezra 10:1-17	1 Cor 6:1-8	31:19-20	11:18-19
20	Ezra 10:18-44	1 Cor 6:9-20	31:21-22	11:20-21
21	Nehemiah 1:1-2:8	1 Cor 7:1-16	31:23-24	11:22
22	Nehemiah 2:9-3:14	1 Cor 7:17-24	32:1-7	11:23
23	Nehemiah 3:15-4:5	1 Cor 7:25-32	32:8-11	11:24-26
24	Nehemiah 4:6-5:13	1 Cor 7:33-40	33:1-5	11:27
25	Nehemiah 5:14-6:19	1 Cor 8:1-3	33:6-11	11:28
26	Nehemiah 7:1-60	1 Cor 8:4-13	33:12-19	11:29-31
27	Nehemiah 7:61-8:18	1 Cor 9:1-10	33:20-22	12:1
28	Nehemiah 9:1-21	1 Cor 9:11-18	34:1-3	12:2-3
29	Nehemiah 9:22-10:27	1 Cor 9:19-27	34:4-10	12:4
30	Nehemiah 10:28-39	1 Cor 10:1-13	34:11-14	12:5-7
31	Nehemiah 11:1-36	1 Cor 10:14-24	34:15-22	12:8-9

APRIL

YEAR TWO

Day	OT	NT	Psalms	Proverbs
☆ 1	Nehemiah 12:1-26	1 Cor 10:25-33	35:1-9	12:10
☆ 2	Nehemiah 12:27-13:14	1 Cor 11:1-12	35:10-18	12:11
☆ 3	Nehemiah 13:15-31	1 Cor 11:13-16	35:19-28	12:12-14
☆ 4	Esther 1:1-2:4	1 Cor 11:17-22	36:1-5	12:15-17
☆ 5	Esther 2:5-3:15	1 Cor 11:23-34	36:6-9	12:18
☆ 6	Esther 4:1-5:14	1 Cor 12:1-7	36:10-12	12:19-20
☆ 7	Esther 6:1-7:10	1 Cor 12:8-26	37:1-6	12:21-23
☆ 8	Esther 8:1-9:15	1 Cor 12:27-31	37:7-11	12:24
☆ 9	Esther 9:16-10:3	1 Cor 13:1-13	37:12-20	12:25
☆ 10	Job 1:1-22	1 Cor 14:1-9	37:21-29	12:26
☆ 11	Job 2:1-3:26	1 Cor 14:10-17	37:30-33	12:27-28
☆ 12	Job 4:1-5:27	1 Cor 14:18-25	37:34-40	13:1
☆ 13	Job 6:1-7:21	1 Cor 14:26-40	38:1-18	13:2-3
☆ 14	Job 8:1-9:24	1 Cor 15:1-11	38:19-22	13:4
☆ 15	Job 9:25-11:20	1 Cor 15:12-28	39:1-5	13:5-6
☆ 16	Job 12:1-13:28	1 Cor 15:29-44	39:6-13	13:7-8
☆ 17	Job 14:1-15:35	1 Cor 15:45-58	40:1-3	13:9-10
☆ 18	Job 16:1-18:4	1 Cor 16:1-9	40:4-10	13:11
☆ 19	Job 18:5-19:29	1 Cor 16:10-24	40:11-13	13:12-14
☆ 20	Job 20:1-21:21	2 Cor 1:1-7	40:14-17	13:15-16
☆ 21	Job 21:22-22:30	2 Cor 1:8-11	41:1-3	13:17-19
☆ 22	Job 23:1-24:25	2 Cor 1:12-22	41:4-13	13:20-23
☆ 23	Job 25:1-27:23	2 Cor 1:23-2:11	42:1-8	13:24-25
☆ 24	Job 28:1-29:17	2 Cor 2:12-14	42:9-11	14:1-2
☆ 25	Job 29:18-30:31	2 Cor 2:15-17	43:1-4	14:3-4
☆ 26	Job 31:1-32:1	2 Cor 3:1-11	43:5	14:5-6
☆ 27	Job 32:2-33:33	2 Cor 3:12-18	44:1-3	14:7-8
☆ 28	Job 34:1-37	2 Cor 4:1-4	44:4-7	14:9-10
☆ 29	Job 35:1-36:33	2 Cor 4:5-12	44:8-22	14:11-12
☆ 30	Job 37:1-24	2 Cor 4:13-18	44:23-26	14:13-14

MAY

YEAR TWO

	Day	OT	NT	Psalms	Proverbs
☆	1	Job 38:1-39:30	2 Cor 5:1-10	45:1-6	14:15-16
☆	2	Job 40:1-41:34	2 Cor 5:11-14	45:7-17	14:17-19
☆	3	Job 42:1-17	2 Cor 5:15-21	46:1-7	14:20-21
☆	4	Ecclesiastes 1:1-2:23	2 Cor 6:1-2	46:8-11	14:22-24
☆	5	Ecclesiastes 2:24-3:22	2 Cor 6:3-13	47:1-7	14:25
☆	6	Ecclesiastes 4:1-5:9	2 Cor 6:14-7:1	47:8-9	14:26-27
☆	7	Ecclesiastes 5:10-6:12	2 Cor 7:2-7	48:1-8	14:28-29
☆	8	Ecclesiastes 7:1-8:8	2 Cor 7:8-10	48:9-14	14:30-31
☆	9	Ecclesiastes 8:9-9:18	2 Cor 7:11-16	49:1-9	14:32-33
☆	10	Ecclesiastes 10:1-11:10	2 Cor 8:1-9	49:10-20	14:34-35
☆	11	Ecclesiastes 12:1-14	2 Cor 8:10-15	50:1-6	15:1-3
☆	12	Song of Songs 1:1-2:17	2 Cor 8:16-20	50:7-23	15:4
☆	13	Song of Songs 3:1-4:16	2 Cor 8:21-24	51:1-9	15:5-7
☆	14	Song of Songs 5:1-6:13	2 Cor 9:1-8	51:10-19	15:8-10
☆	15	Song of Songs 7:1-8:14	2 Cor 9:9-15	52:1-7	15:11
☆	16	Isaiah 1:1-31	2 Cor 10:1-12	52:8-9	15:12-14
☆	17	Isaiah 2:1-22	2 Cor 10:13-18	53:1-5	15:15-17
☆	18	Isaiah 3:1-4:6	2 Cor 11:1-6	53:6	15:18-19
☆	19	Isaiah 5:1-30	2 Cor 11:7-15	54:1-4	15:20-21
☆	20	Isaiah 6:1-7:9	2 Cor 11:16-21	54:5-7	15:22-23
☆	21	Isaiah 7:10-25	2 Cor 11:22-33	55:1-11	15:24-26
☆	22	Isaiah 8:1-22	2 Cor 12:1-7	55:12-23	15:27-28
☆	23	Isaiah 9:1-21	2 Cor 12:8-10	56:1-9	15:29-30
☆	24	Isaiah 10:1-23	2 Cor 12:11-15	56:10-13	15:31-32
☆	25	Isaiah 10:24-11:16	2 Cor 12:16-21	57:1-3	15:33
☆	26	Isaiah 12:1-14:2	2 Cor 13:1-6	57:4-11	16:1-3
☆	27	Isaiah 14:3-32	2 Cor 13:7-14	58:1-9	16:4-5
☆	28	Isaiah 15:1-16:14	Galatians 1:1-10	58:10-11	16:6-7
☆	29	Isaiah 17:1-18:7	Galatians 1:11-24	59:1-13	16:8-9
☆	30	Isaiah 19:1-25	Galatians 2:1-10	59:14-17	16:10-11
☆	31	Isaiah 20:1-21:17	Galatians 2:11-16	60:1-5	16:12-13

JUNE

YEAR TWO

Day	OT	NT	Psalms	Proverbs
☆ 1	Isaiah 22:1-25	Galatians 2:17-21	60:6-12	16:14-15
☆ 2	Isaiah 23:1-24:23	Galatians 3:1-9	61:1-3	16:16-17
☆ 3	Isaiah 25:1-26:21	Galatians 3:10-14	61:4-8	16:18
☆ 4	Isaiah 27:1-28:13	Galatians 3:15-22	62:1-8	16:19-20
☆ 5	Isaiah 28:14-29:14	Galatians 3:23-4:20	62:9-12	16:21-23
☆ 6	Isaiah 29:15-30:11	Galatians 4:21-31	63:1-5	16:24
☆ 7	Isaiah 30:12-31:9	Galatians 5:1-6	63:6-11	16:25
☆ 8	Isaiah 32:1-33:9	Galatians 5:7-12	64:1-9	16:26-27
☆ 9	Isaiah 33:10-35:10	Galatians 5:13-18	64:10	16:28-30
☆ 10	Isaiah 36:1-22	Galatians 5:19-26	65:1-4	16:31-33
☆ 11	Isaiah 37:1-29	Galatians 6:1-10	65:5-13	17:1
☆ 12	Isaiah 37:30-38:22	Galatians 6:11-18	66:1-7	17:2-3
☆ 13	Isaiah 39:1-40:17	Ephesians 1:1-14	66:8-20	17:4-5
☆ 14	Isaiah 40:18-41:16	Ephesians 1:15-23	67:1-3	17:6
☆ 15	Isaiah 41:17-42:9	Ephesians 2:1-10	67:4-7	17:7-8
☆ 16	Isaiah 42:10-43:13	Ephesians 2:11-22	68:1-6	17:9-11
☆ 17	Isaiah 43:14-44:8	Ephesians 3:1-11	68:7-18	17:12-13
☆ 18	Isaiah 44:9-45:10	Ephesians 3:12-21	68:19-31	17:14-15
☆ 19	Isaiah 45:11-46:13	Ephesians 4:1-8	68:32-35	17:16
☆ 20	Isaiah 47:1-48:11	Ephesians 4:9-16	69:1-13	17:17-18
☆ 21	Isaiah 48:12-49:12	Ephesians 4:17-24	69:14-18	17:19-21
☆ 22	Isaiah 49:13-50:11	Ephesians 4:25-32	69:19-31	17:22
☆ 23	Isaiah 51:1-23	Ephesians 5:1-9	69:32-36	17:23
☆ 24	Isaiah 52:1-53:12	Ephesians 5:10-33	70:1-5	17:24-25
☆ 25	Isaiah 54:1-55:13	Ephesians 6:1-9	71:1-6	17:26
☆ 26	Isaiah 56:1-57:14	Ephesians 6:10-24	71:7-16	17:27-28
☆ 27	Isaiah 57:15-58:14	Philippians 1:1-11	71:17-24	18:1
☆ 28	Isaiah 59:1-21	Philippians 1:12-26	72:1-14	18:2-3
☆ 29	Isaiah 60:1-22	Philippians 1:27-2:2	72:15-20	18:4-5
☆ 30	Isaiah 61:1-62:5	Philippians 2:3-18	73:1-20	18:6-7

JULY

YEAR TWO

Day	OT	NT	Psalms	Proverbs
☆ 1	Isaiah 62:6-64:12	Philippians 2:19-30	73:21-28	18:8
☆ 2	Isaiah 65:1-25	Philippians 3:1-3	74:1-11	18:9-10
☆ 3	Isaiah 66:1-9	Philippians 3:4-12	74:12-23	18:11-12
☆ 4	Isaiah 66:10-24	Philippians 3:13-21	75:1-5	18:13
☆ 5	Jeremiah 1:1-19	Philippians 4:1-7	75:6-10	18:14-15
☆ 6	Jeremiah 2:1-30	Philippians 4:8-23	76:1-7	18:16-18
☆ 7	Jeremiah 2:31-3:20	Colossians 1:1-10	76:8-12	18:19
☆ 8	Jeremiah 3:21-4:18	Colossians 1:11-17	77:1-14	18:20-21
☆ 9	Jeremiah 4:19-5:19	Colossians 1:18-27	77:15-20	18:22
☆ 10	Jeremiah 5:20-6:15	Colossians 1:28-2:7	78:1-22	18:23-24
☆ 11	Jeremiah 6:16-7:20	Colossians 2:8-12	78:23-31	19:1-3
☆ 12	Jeremiah 7:21-8:7	Colossians 2:13-23	78:32-39	19:4-5
☆ 13	Jeremiah 8:8-22	Colossians 3:1-11	78:40-55	19:6-7
☆ 14	Jeremiah 9:1-26	Colossians 3:12-17	78:56-59	19:8-9
☆ 15	Jeremiah 10:1-25	Colossians 3:18-4:6	78:60-64	19:10-12
☆ 16	Jeremiah 11:1-23	Colossians 4:7-18	78:65-69	19:13-14
☆ 17	Jeremiah 12:1-13:7	1 Thess 1:1-10	78:70-72	19:15-16
☆ 18	Jeremiah 13:8-14-10	1 Thess 2:1-8	79:1-8	19:17
☆ 19	Jeremiah 14:11-15:9	1 Thess 2:9-16	79:9-13	19:18-19
☆ 20	Jeremiah 15:10-16:15	1 Thess 2:17-3:13	80:1-13	19:20-21
☆ 21	Jeremiah 16:16-17:27	1 Thess 4:1-12	80:14-19	19:22-23
☆ 22	Jeremiah 18:1-23	1 Thess 4:13-5:3	81:1-7	19:24-25
☆ 23	Jeremiah 19:1-20:6	1 Thess 5:4-11	81:8-16	19-26
☆ 24	Jeremiah 20:7-21:14	1 Thess 5:12-28	82:1-5	19:27-29
☆ 25	Jeremiah 22:1-30	2 Thess 1:1-6	82:6-8	20:1
☆ 26	Jeremiah 23:1-20	2 Thess 1:7-12	83:1-8	20:2-3
☆ 27	Jeremiah 23:21-24:10	2 Thess 2:1-12	83:9-18	20:4-6
☆ 28	Jeremiah 25:1-38	2 Thess 2:13-17	84:1-4	20:7
☆ 29	Jeremiah 26:1-24	2 Thess 3:1-5	84:5-12	20:8-10
☆ 30	Jeremiah 27:1-22	2 Thess 3:6-18	85:1-7	20:11
☆ 31	Jeremiah 28:1-17	1 Timothy 1:1-11	85:8-13	20:12

AUGUST

YEAR TWO

Day	OT	NT	Psalms	Proverbs
1	Jeremiah 29:1-32	1 Timothy 1:12-20	86:1-7	20:13-15
2	Jeremiah 30:1-24	1 Timothy 2:1-7	86:8-17	20:16-18
3	Jeremiah 31:1-26	1 Timothy 2:8-15	87:1-3	20:19
4	Jeremiah 31:27-32:5	1 Timothy 3:1-5	87:4-7	20:20-21
5	Jeremiah 32:6-44	1 Timothy 3:6-16	88:1-12	20:22-23
6	Jeremiah 33:1-22	1 Timothy 4:1-6	88:13-18	20:24-25
7	Jeremiah 33:23-34:22	1 Timothy 4:7-16	89:1-6	20:26-27
8	Jeremiah 35:1-19	1 Timothy 5:1-16	89:7-13	20:28-30
9	Jeremiah 36:1-32	1 Timothy 5:17-25	89:14-18	21:1-2
10	Jeremiah 37:1-21	1 Timothy 6:1-11	89:19-37	21:3
11	Jeremiah 38:1-28	1 Timothy 6:12-21	89:38-46	21:4
12	Jeremiah 39:1-40:6	2 Timothy 1:1-8	89:47-52	21:5-7
13	Jeremiah 40:7-41:18	2 Timothy 1:9-18	90:1-17	21:8-10
14	Jeremiah 42:1-43:13	2 Timothy 2:1-7	91:1-16	21:11-12
15	Jeremiah 44:1-23	2 Timothy 2:8-21	92:1-15	21:13
16	Jeremiah 44:24-46:12	2 Timothy 2:22-26	93:1-5	21:14-16
17	Jeremiah 46:13-47:7	2 Timothy 3:1-17	94:1-13	21:17-18
18	Jeremiah 48:1-47	2 Timothy 4:1-5	94:14-23	21:19-20
19	Jeremiah 49:1-22	2 Timothy 4:6-22	95:1-11	21:21-22
20	Jeremiah 49:23-50:20	Titus 1:1-3	96:1-13	21:23-24
21	Jeremiah 50:21-46	Titus 1:4-16	97:1-12	21:25-26
22	Jeremiah 51:1-26	Titus 2:1-8	98:1-9	21:27
23	Jeremiah 51:27-53	Titus 2:9-15	99:1-4	21:28-29
24	Jeremiah 51:54-52:11	Titus 3:1-8	99:5-9	21:30-31
25	Jeremiah 52:12-34	Titus 3:9-15	100:1-2	22:1
26	Lamentations 1:1-22	Philemon 1:1-3	100:3-5	22:2-4
27	Lamentations 2:1-19	Philemon 1:4-25	101:1-3	22:5-6
28	Lamentations 2:20-3:24	Hebrews 1:1-8	101:4-8	22:7
29	Lamentations 3:25-66	Hebrews 1:9-14	102:1-17	22:8-9
30	Lamentations 4:1-22	Hebrews 2:1-13	102:18-22	22:10-12
31	Lamentations 5:1-22	Hebrews 2:14-18	102:23-28	22:13

SEPTEMBER

YEAR TWO

Day	OT	NT	Psalms	Proverbs
1	Ezekiel 1:1-28	Hebrews 3:1-12	103:1-12	22:14
2	Ezekiel 2:1-3:15	Hebrews 3:13-19	103:13-22	22:15
3	Ezekiel 3:16-4:17	Hebrews 4:1-11	104:1-7	22:16
4	Ezekiel 5:1-6:14	Hebrews 4:12-16	104:8-23	22:17-19
5	Ezekiel 7:1-27	Hebrews 5:1-11	104:24-30	22:20-21
6	Ezekiel 8:1-9:11	Hebrews 5:12-14	104:31-35	22:22-23
7	Ezekiel 10:1-22	Hebrews 6:1-10	105:1-7	22:24-25
8	Ezekiel 11:1-25	Hebrews 6:11-20	105:8-15	22:26-27
9	Ezekiel 12:1-28	Hebrews 7:1-10	105:16-26	22:28-29
10	Ezekiel 13:1-14:11	Hebrews 7:11-17	105:27-36	23:1-3
11	Ezekiel 14:12-15:8	Hebrews 7:18-25	105:37-45	23:4-5
12	Ezekiel 16:1-41	Hebrews 7:26-28	106:1-2	23:6-8
13	Ezekiel 16:42-63	Hebrews 8:1-6	106:3-5	23:9-11
14	Ezekiel 17:1-24	Hebrews 8:7-13	106:6-12	23:12
15	Ezekiel 18:1-32	Hebrews 9:1-5	106:13-23	23:13-14
16	Ezekiel 19:1-14	Hebrews 9:6-10	106:24-31	23:15-16
17	Ezekiel 20:1-26	Hebrews 9:11-23	106:32-46	23:17-18
18	Ezekiel 20:27-49	Hebrews 9:24-28	106:47-48	23:19-21
19	Ezekiel 21:1-32	Hebrews 10:1-7	107:1-3	23:22
20	Ezekiel 22:1-31	Hebrews 10:8-17	107:4-32	23:23
21	Ezekiel 23:1-27	Hebrews 10:18-23	107:33-43	23:24
22	Ezekiel 23:28-49	Hebrews 10:24-39	108:1-4	23:25-28
23	Ezekiel 24:1-25:11	Hebrews 11:1-7	108:5-13	23:29-35
24	Ezekiel 25:12-26:21	Hebrews 11:8-16	109:1-21	24:1-2
25	Ezekiel 27:1-36	Hebrews 11:17-23	109:22-31	24:3-4
26	Ezekiel 28:1-26	Hebrews 11:24-31	110:1-3	24:5-6
27	Ezekiel 29:1-21	Hebrews 11:32-40	110:4-7	24:7
28	Ezekiel 30:1-26	Hebrews 12:1-13	111:1-4	24:8
29	Ezekiel 31:1-18	Hebrews 12:14-24	111:5-10	24:9-10
30	Ezekiel 32:1-32	Hebrews 12:25-29	112:1-3	24:11-12

OCTOBER

YEAR TWO

Day	OT	NT	Psalms	Proverbs
☆ 1	Ezekiel 33:1-33	Hebrews 13:1-16	112:4-10	24:13-14
☆ 2	Ezekiel 34:1-31	Hebrews 13:17-25	113:1-9	24:15-16
☆ 3	Ezekiel 35:1-36:15	James 1:1-8	114:1-8	24:17-20
☆ 4	Ezekiel 36:16-38	James 1:9-18	115:1-10	24:21-22
☆ 5	Ezekiel 37:1-28	James 1:19-27	115:11-18	24:23-25
☆ 6	Ezekiel 38:1-23	James 2:1-17	116:1-5	24:26
☆ 7	Ezekiel 39:1-29	James 2:18-3:6	116:6-14	24:27
☆ 8	Ezekiel 40:1-27	James 3:7-18	116:15-117:2	24:28-29
☆ 9	Ezekiel 40:28-49	James 4:1-10	118:1-7	24:30-34
☆ 10	Ezekiel 41:1-26	James 4:11-17	118:8-18	25:1-5
☆ 11	Ezekiel 42:1-43:4	James 5:1-8	118:19-26	25:6-8
☆ 12	Ezekiel 43:5-27	James 5:9-20	118:27-29	25:9-10
☆ 13	Ezekiel 44:1-31	1 Peter 1:1-6	119:1-8	25:11-14
☆ 14	Ezekiel 45:1-12	1 Peter 1:7-12	119:9-16	25:15
☆ 15	Ezekiel 45:13-46:3	1 Peter 1:13-25	119:17-24	25:16
☆ 16	Ezekiel 46:4-24	1 Peter 2:1-10	119:25-32	25:17
☆ 17	Ezekiel 47:1-23	1 Peter.2:11-25	119:33-40	25:18-19
☆ 18	Ezekiel 48:1-35	1 Peter 3:1-7	119:41-48	25:20-22
☆ 19	Daniel 1:1-21	1 Peter 3:8-22	119:49-58	25:23-24
☆ 20	Daniel 2:1-23	1 Peter 4:1-6	119:59-64	25:25-27
☆ 21	Daniel 2:24-49	1 Peter 4:7-19	119:65-72	25:28
☆ 22	Daniel 3:1-30	1 Peter 5:1-14	119:73-80	26:1-2
☆ 23	Daniel 4:1-27	2 Peter 1:1-9	119:81-88	26:3-5
☆ 24	Daniel 4:28-37	2 Peter 1:10-21	119:89-96	26:6-8
☆ 25	Daniel 5:1-12	2 Peter 2:1-10	119:97-104	26:9-12
☆ 26	Daniel 5:13-31	2 Peter 2:11-22	119-105-112	26:13-16
☆ 27	Daniel 6:1-18	2 Peter 3:1-11	119:113-120	26:17
☆ 28	Daniel 6:19-28	2 Peter 3:12-18	119:121-128	26:18-19
☆ 29	Daniel 7:1-14	1 John 1:1-4	119:129-136	26:20
☆ 30	Daniel 7:15-28	1 John 1:5-10	119:137-152	26:21-22
☆ 31	Daniel 8:1-14	1 John 2:1-6	119:153-159	26:23

NOVEMBER

YEAR TWO

Day	OT	NT	Psalms	Proverbs
1	Daniel 8:15-27	1 John 2:7-17	119:160-168	26:24-26
2	Daniel 9:1-27	1 John 2:18-29	119:169-175	26:27
3	Daniel 10:1-11:1	1 John 3:1-6	120:1-7	26:28
4	Daniel 11:2-12	1 John 3:7-13	121:1-4	27:1-2
5	Daniel 11:13-35	1 John 3:14-24	121:5-8	27:3
6	Daniel 11:36-45	1 John 4:1-6	122:1-5	27:4-6
7	Daniel 12:1-13	1 John 4:7-21	122:6-9	27:7-9
8	Hosea 1:1-2:1	1 John 5:1-12	123:1-2	27:10
9	Hosea 2:2-3:5	1 John 5:13-21	123:3-4	27:11
10	Hosea 4:1-19	2 John 1:1-6	124:1-6	27:12
11	Hosea 5:1-15	2 John 1:7-13	124:7-8	27:13
12	Hosea 6:1-7:16	3 John 1:1-4	125:1-3	27:14
13	Hosea 8:1-9:17	3 John 1:5-15	125:4-5	27:15-16
14	Hosea 10:1-11:12	Jude 1:1-19	126:1-3	27:17
15	Hosea 12:1-14:9	Jude 1:20-25	126:4-6	27:18-20
16	Joel 1:1-2:32	Revelation 1:1-8	127:1-2	27:21-22
17	Joel 3:1-21	Revelation 1:9-20	127:3-5	27:23-27
18	Amos 1:1-15	Revelation 2:1-7	128:1-4	28:1
19	Amos 2:1-3:15	Revelation 2:8-17	128-5-6	28:2
20	Amos 4:1-5:9	Revelation 2:18-29	129:1-4	28:3-5
21	Amos 5:10-6:14	Revelation 3:1-6	129:5-8	28:6-7
22	Amos 7:1-8:3	Revelation 3:7-13	130:1-5	28:8-10
23	Amos 8:4-9:15	Revelation 3:14-22	130:6-8	28:11
24	Obadiah 1:1-14	Revelation 4:1-6	131:1-132:9	28:12-13
25	Obadiah 1:15-21	Revelation 4:7-11	132:10-12	28:14
26	Jonah 1:1-2:10	Revelation 5:1-8	132:13-18	28:15-16
27	Jonah 3:1-4:11	Revelation 5:9-14	133:1-2	28:17-18
28	Micah 1:1-2:13	Revelation 6:1-8	133:3	28:19-20
29	Micah 3:1-4:13	Revelation 6:9-17	134:1-135:4	28:21-22
30	Micah 5:1-6:8	Revelation 7:1-8	135:5-12	28:23-24

DECEMBER

YEAR TWO

Day	OT	NT	Psalms	Proverbs
1	Micah 6:9-7:20	Revelation 7:9-17	135:13-21	28:25-26
2	Nahum 1:1-2:13	Revelation 8:1-5	136:1-12	28:27-28
3	Nahum 3:1-19	Revelation 8:6-13	136:13-26	29:1
4	Habakkuk 1:1-2:11	Revelation 9:1-12	137:1-4	29:2-4
5	Habakkuk 2:12-3:19	Revelation 9:13-21	137:5-9	29:5-8
6	Zephaniah 1:1-2:15	Revelation 10:1-7	138:1-6	29:9-11
7	Zephaniah 3:1-20	Revelation 10:8-11	138:7-8	29:12-14
8	Haggai 1:1-15	Revelation 11:1-14	139:1-12	29:15-17
9	Haggai 2:1-23	Revelation 11:15-19	139:13-24	29:18
10	Zechariah 1:1-13	Revelation 12:1-9	140:1-8	29:19-20
11	Zechariah 1:14-21	Revelation 12:10-17	140:9-13	29:21-22
12	Zechariah 2:1-13	Revelation 12:18-13:10	141:1-2	29:23
13	Zechariah 3:1-10	Revelation 13:11-18	141:3-10	29:24-25
14	Zechariah 4:1-14	Revelation 14:1-12	142:1-3	29:26-27
15	Zechariah 5:1-11	Revelation 14:13-20	142:4-7	30:1-4
16	Zechariah 6:1-15	Revelation 15:1-4	143:1-6	30:5-6
17	Zechariah 7:1-14	Revelation 15:5-8	143:7-12	30:7-9
18	Zechariah 8:1-13	Revelation 16:1-11	144:1-8	30:10
19	Zechariah 8:14-23	Revelation 16:12-21	144:9-15	30:11-14
20	Zechariah 9:1-8	Revelation 17:1-8	145:1-7	30:15-16
21	Zechariah 9:9-17	Revelation 17:9-18	145:8-21	30:17
22	Zechariah 10:1-12	Revelation 18:1-10	146:1-2	30:18-20
23	Zechariah 11:1-17	Revelation 18:11-24	146:3-10	30:21-23
24	Zechariah 12:1-14	Revelation 19:1-10	147:1-11	30:24-28
25	Zechariah 13:1-9	Revelation 19:11-21	147:12-20	30:29-31
26	Zechariah 14:1-11	Revelation 20:1-10	148:1-4	30:32
27	Zechariah 14:12-21	Revelation 20:11-15	148:5-14	30:33
28	Malachi 1:1-14	Revelation 21:1-14	149:1	31:1-7
29	Malachi 2:1-17	Revelation 21:15-27	149:2-9	31:8-9
30	Malachi 3:1-18	Revelation 22:1-7	150:1-5	31:10-24
31	Malachi 4:1-6	Revelation 22:8-21	150:6	31:25-31

Daily
JOURNAL
PAGES

DRAW WHAT GOD iS SHOWiNG YOU

Write what God is SAYING

DRAW
WHAT
GOD IS
SHOWING
YOU

Write what God is SAYING

draw what
God is showing you

Write what God is SAYING

draw what God is
showing you

Write what God is
SAYING

DRAW
WHAT
GOD IS
SHOWING
YOU

Write what God is SAYING

DRAW WHAT GOD iS SHOWiNG YOU

Write what God is SAYING

DRAW WHAT GOD IS SHOWING YOU

Write what God is SAYING

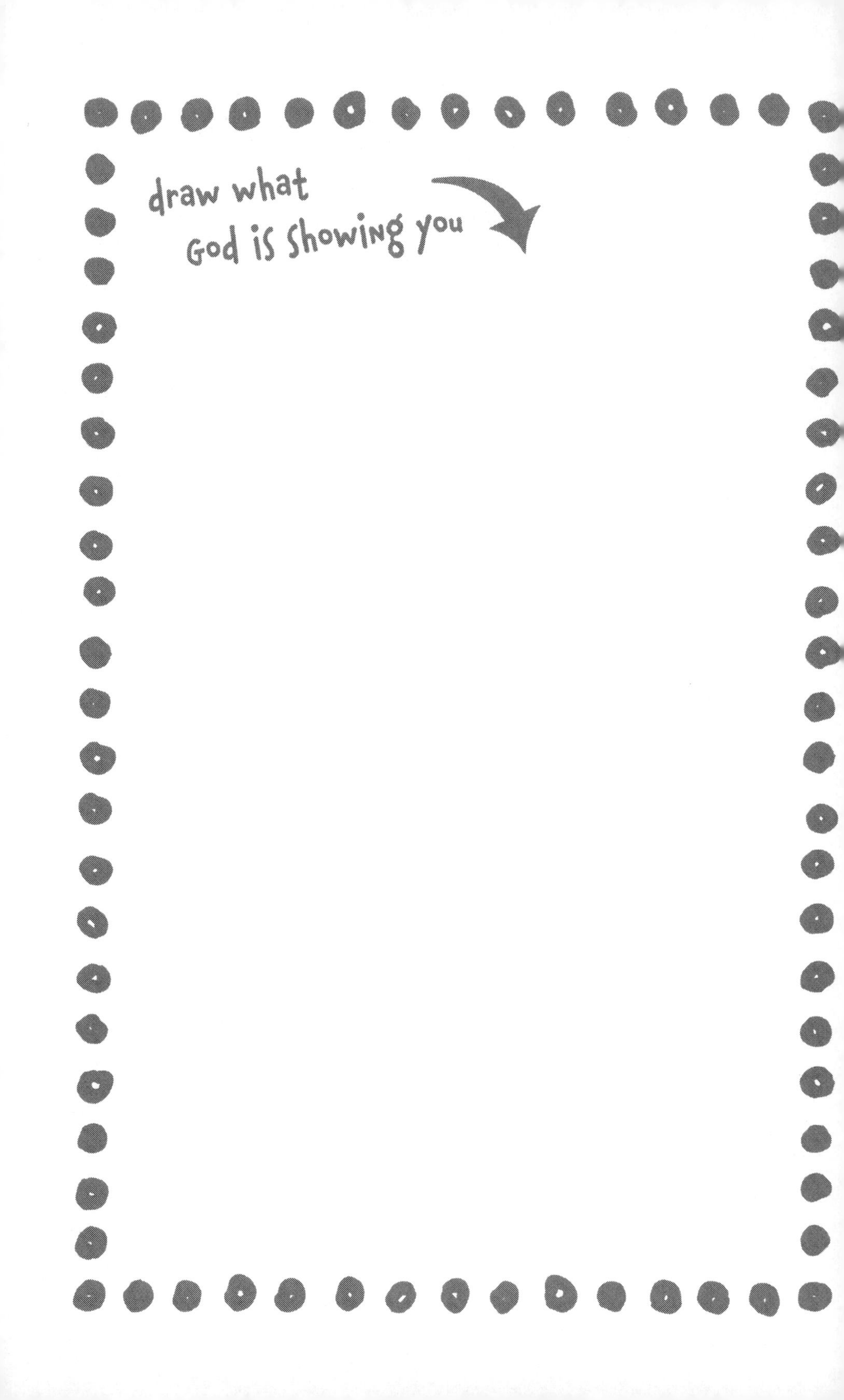
draw what
God is Showing you

Write what God is SAYING

draw what God is
showing you

Write what God is
SAYING

DRAW WHAT GOD IS SHOWING YOU

Write what God is SAYING

DRAW WHAT GOD iS SHOWiNG YOU

Write what God is SAYING

DRAW WHAT GOD IS SHOWING YOU

Write what God is SAYING

draw what
God is showing you

Write what God is SAYING

draw what God is
showing you

Write what God is
SAYING

DRAW
WHAT
GOD IS
SHOWING
YOU

Write what God is SAYING

DRAW WHAT GOD iS SHOWiNG YOU

Write what God is SAYING

DRAW
WHAT
GOD IS
SHOWING
YOU

Write what God is SAYING

draw what
God is showing you

Write what God is SAYING

draw what God is
showing you

Write what God is
SAYING

DRAW
WHAT
GOD IS
SHOWING
YOU

Write what God is SAYING

DRAW WHAT GOD iS SHOWiNG YOU

Write what God is SAYING

DRAW WHAT GOD IS SHOWING YOU

Write what God is SAYING

draw what
God is showing you

Write what God is SAYING

draw what God is
showing you

Write what God is
SAYING

DRAW
WHAT
GOD IS
SHOWING
YOU

Write what God is SAYING

DRAW WHAT GOD iS SHOWiNG YOU

Write what God is SAYING

DRAW WHAT GOD IS SHOWING YOU

Write what God is SAYING

draw what
God is showing you

Write what God is SAYING

draw what God is
showing you

Write what God is
SAYING

DRAW
WHAT
GOD IS
SHOWING
YOU

Write what God is SAYING

DRAW WHAT GOD iS SHOWiNG YOU

Write what God is SAYING

DRAW WHAT GOD IS SHOWING YOU

Write what God is SAYING

draw what
God is showing you

Write what God is SAYING

draw what God is
showing you

Write what God is
SAYING

DRAW
WHAT
GOD IS
SHOWING
YOU

Write what God is SAYING

DRAW WHAT GOD iS SHOWiNG YOU

Write what God is SAYING

DRAW
WHAT
GOD IS
SHOWING
YOU

Write what God is SAYING

draw what
God is showing you

Write what God is SAYING

draw what God is
showing you

Write what God is
SAYING

DRAW
WHAT
GOD IS
SHOWING
YOU

Write what God is SAYING

DRAW WHAT GOD iS SHOWiNG YOU

Write what God is SAYING

DRAW WHAT GOD IS SHOWING YOU

Write what God is

SAYING

draw what
God is showing you

Write what God is SAYING

draw what God is
showing you

Write what God is
SAYING

DRAW
WHAT
GOD IS
SHOWING
YOU

Write what God is SAYING

DRAW WHAT GOD iS SHOWiNG YOU

Write what God is SAYING

DRAW
WHAT
GOD IS
SHOWING
YOU

Write what God is SAYING

draw what
God is showing you

Write what God is SAYING

draw what God is
showing you

Write what God is
SAYING

DRAW
WHAT
GOD IS
SHOWING
YOU

Write what God is SAYING

DRAW WHAT GOD iS SHOWiNG YOU

Write what God is SAYING

DRAW
WHAT
GOD IS
SHOWING
YOU

Write what God is SAYING

draw what
God is showing you

Write what God is SAYING

draw what God is
showing you

Write what God is
SAYING

DRAW
WHAT
GOD IS
SHOWING
YOU

Write what God is SAYING

DRAW WHAT GOD iS SHOWiNG YOU

Write what God is SAYING

DRAW
WHAT
GOD IS
SHOWING
YOU

Write what God is SAYING

draw what
God is showing you

Write what God is SAYING

draw what God is
showing you

Write what God is
SAYING

(a fancy word that means "extra stuff at the end")

APPENDIX:

SCRIPTURES FOR COMMON PRAYER NEEDS

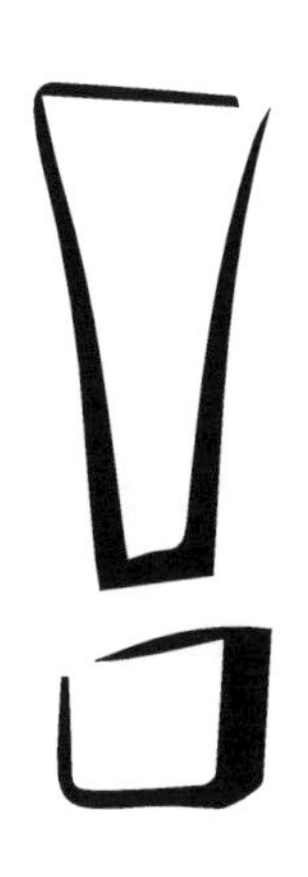

APPENDIX:
SCRIPTURES FOR COMMON PRAYER NEEDS

When we pray Scripture, we say that we agree with the truth of God's Word. In this section, many common prayer needs have been listed with passages of scripture to help you as you pray.

Family

God provides homes for those who are deserted.
He leads out the prisoners to prosperity,
but the rebellious live in a scorched land. **(Psalm 68:6)**

And he will turn the hearts of fathers to their children and the hearts of children to their fathers. Otherwise, I will come and strike the land with a curse." **(Malachi 4:6)**

Children, obey your parents in the Lord, because this is right. Honor your father and mother, which is the first commandment with a promise, so that it may go well with you and that you may have a long life in the land. **(Ephesians 6:1-3)**

Children, obey your parents in everything, for this pleases the Lord. **(Colossians 3:20)**

Fear

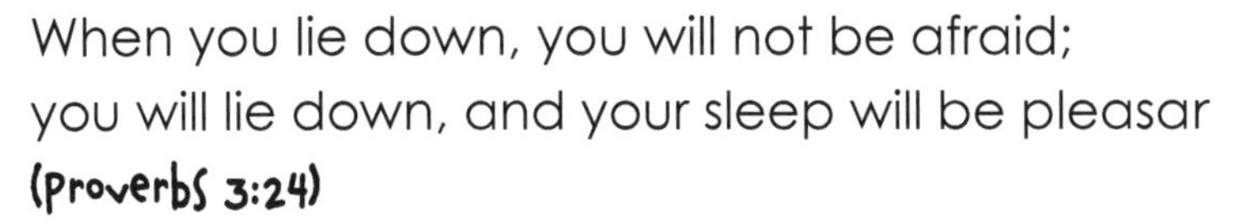

When you lie down, you will not be afraid;
you will lie down, and your sleep will be pleasar

(Proverbs 3:24)

Protect me as the pupil of your eye;
hide me in the shadow of your wings. (Psalm 17:8)

For God has not given us a spirit of fear, but one of power, love, and sound judgment. (2 Timothy 1:7)

Because you have made the Lord—my refuge,
the Most High—your dwelling place, no harm will come to you; no plague will come near your tent.
(Psalm 91:9-10)

For you did not receive a spirit of slavery to fall back into fear. Instead, you received the Spirit of adoption, by whom we cry out, "*Abba*, Father!" (Romans 8:15)

Friendship

I am a friend to all who fear you,
to those who keep your precepts. (Psalm 119:63)

A friend loves at all times,
and a brother is born for a difficult time. (Proverbs 17:17)

"By this everyone will know that you are my disciples, if you love one another." (John 13:35)

Can two walk together
without agreeing to meet? (Amos 3:3)

This is what I command you: Love one another.
(John 15:17)

Iron sharpens iron,
and one person sharpens another. (Proverbs 27:17)

This is my command: Love one another as I have loved you. No one has greater love than this: to lay down his life for his friends. You are my friends if you do what I command you. (John 15:12-14)

And if someone overpowers one person, two can resist him. A cord of three strands is not easily broken.
(Ecclesiastes 4:12)

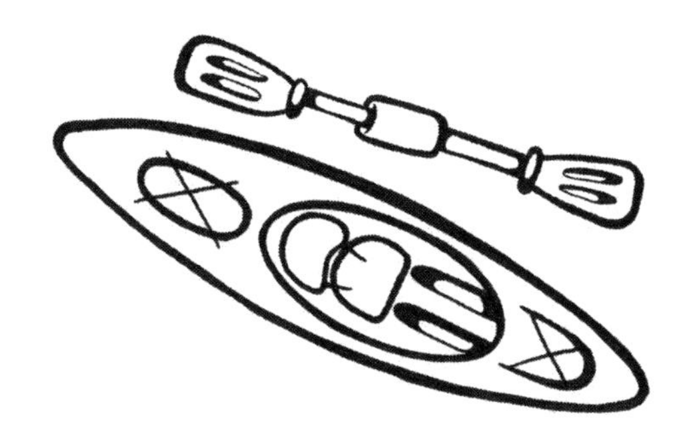

Healing

But he was pierced because of our rebellion,
crushed because of our iniquities;
punishment for our peace was on him,
and we are healed by his wounds. **(Isaiah 53:5)**

He himself bore our sins in his body on the tree; so that, having died to sins, we might live for righteousness. By his wounds you have been healed. **(1 Peter 2:24)**

As you go, proclaim: 'The kingdom of heaven has come near.' Heal the sick, raise the dead, cleanse those with leprosy, drive out demons. Freely you received, freely give. **(Matthew 10:7-8)**

"And these signs will accompany those who believe: In my name they will drive out demons; they will speak in new tongues; they will pick up snakes; if they should drink anything deadly, it will not harm them; they will lay hands on the sick, and they will get well." **(Mark 16:17-18)**

He said, "If you will carefully obey the Lord your God, do what is right in his sight, pay attention to his commands, and keep all his statutes, I will not inflict any illnesses on you that I inflicted on the Egyptians. For I am the Lord who heals you." **(Exodus 15:26)**

... how God anointed Jesus of Nazareth with the Holy Spirit and with power, and how he went about doing good and healing all who were under the tyranny of the devil, because God was with him. **(Acts 10:38)**

Loving Others

For this reason I kneel before the Father from whom every family in heaven and on earth is named. I pray that he may grant you, according to the riches of his glory, to be strengthened with power in your inner being through his Spirit, and that Christ may dwell in your hearts through faith. I pray that you, being rooted and firmly established in love, may be able to comprehend with all the saints what is the length and width, height and depth of God's love, and to know Christ's love that surpasses knowledge, so that you may be filled with all the fullness of God. **(Ephesians 3:14-19)**

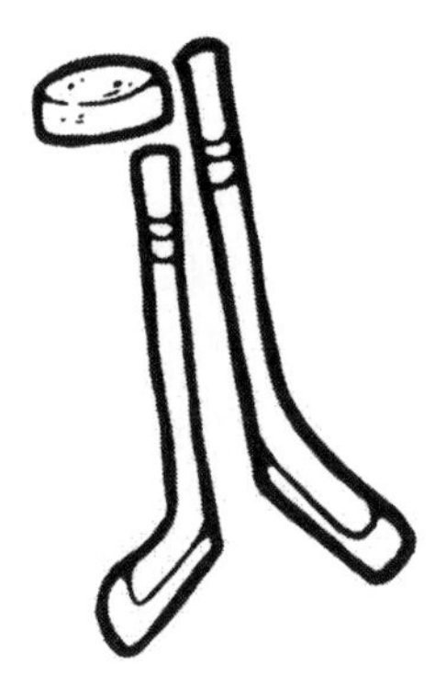

Dear friends, let us love one another, because love is from God, and everyone who loves has been born of God and knows God. **(1 John 4:7)**

Little children, let us not love in word or speech, but in action and in truth. **(1 John 3:18)**

But I tell you, love your enemies and pray for those who persecute you, so that you may be children of your Father in heaven. For he causes his sun to rise on the evil and the good, and sends rain on the righteous and the unrighteous. **(Matthew 5:44-45)**

Finally, all of you be like-minded and sympathetic, love one another, and be compassionate and humble,
(1 Peter 3:8)

By this everyone will know that you are my disciples, if you love one another. **(John 13:35)**

Therefore, as God's chosen ones, holy
and dearly loved, put on compassion,
kindness, humility, gentleness, and patience, bearing with one another and forgiving one another if anyone has a grievance against another. Just as the Lord has forgiven you, so you are also to forgive. Above all, put on love, which is the perfect bond of unity.
(Colossians 3:12-14)

Obedience

"The one who has my commands and keeps them is the one who loves me. And the one who loves me will be loved by my Father. I also will love him and will reveal myself to him." (John 14:21)

Jesus replied, "Truly I tell you, the Son is not able to do anything on his own, but only what he sees the Father doing. For whatever the Father does, the Son likewise does these things. (John 5:19)

Anyone who is not with me is against me, and anyone who does not gather with me scatters. (Luke 11:23)

"Therefore, everyone who hears these words of mine and acts on them will be like a wise man who built his house on the rock." (Matthew 7:24)

Peace

You will keep the mind that is dependent on you in perfect peace, for it is trusting in you. (Isaiah 26:3)

"Peace I leave with you. My peace I give to you. I do not give to you as the world gives. Don't let your heart be troubled or fearful." (John 14:27)

Don't worry about anything, but in everything, through prayer and petition with thanksgiving, present your requests to God. And the peace of God, which surpasses all understanding, will guard your hearts and minds in Christ Jesus. (Philippians 4:6-7)

Blessed are the peacemakers, for they will be called sons of God. (Matthew 5:9)

Glory to God in the highest heaven, and peace on earth to people he favors! (Luke 2:14)

Relationship With God

And I will ask the Father, and he will give you another Counselor to be with you forever. He is the Spirit of truth. The world is unable to receive him because it doesn't see him or know him. But you do know him, because he remains with you and will be in you. (John 14:16-17)

Jesus answered, "If anyone loves me, he will keep my word. My Father will love him, and we will come to him and make our home with him. (John 14:23)

He said to him, "Love the Lord your God with all your heart, with all your soul, and with all your mind. (Matthew 22:37)

I have asked one thing from the Lord;
it is what I desire:
to dwell in the house of the Lord
all the days of my life,
gazing on the beauty of the Lord
and seeking him in his temple. (Psalm 27:4)

For God loved the world in this way: He gave his one and only Son, so that everyone who believes in him will not perish but have eternal life. (John 3:16)

For I am persuaded that neither death nor life, nor angels nor rulers, nor things present nor things to come, nor powers, nor height nor depth, nor any other created thing will be able to separate us from the love of God that is in Christ Jesus our Lord. (Romans 8:38-39)

Safety

I will both lie down and sleep in peace, for you alone, Lord, make me live in safety. (Psalm 4:8)

Indeed, I will certainly deliver you so that you do not fall by the sword. Because you have trusted in me, you will retain your life like the spoils of war. This is the Lord's declaration. (Jeremiah 39:18)

The Lord is a refuge for the persecuted, a refuge in times of trouble. (Psalm 9:9)

You have set my feet in a spacious place. (Psalm 31:8)

The name of the Lord is a strong tower; the righteous run to it and are protected. (Proverbs 18:10)

Now, Father, glorify me in your presence with that glory I had with you before the world existed. (John 17:5)

Unbelievers

First of all, then, I urge that petitions, prayers, intercessions, and thanksgivings be made for everyone, for kings and all those who are in authority, so that we may lead a tranquil and quiet life in all godliness and dignity. This is good, and it pleases God our Savior, who wants everyone to be saved and to come to the knowledge of the truth. (1 Timothy 2:1-4)

For God who said, "Let light shine out of darkness," has shone in our hearts to give the light of the knowledge of God's glory in the face of Jesus Christ. (2 Corinthians 4:6)

In the same way, let your light shine before others, so that they may see your good works and give glory to your Father in heaven. (Matthew 5:16)

When he comes, he will convict the world about sin, righteousness, and judgment: (John 16:8)

For God loved the world in this way: He gave his one and only Son, so that everyone who believes in him will not perish but have eternal life. (John 3:16)

Conduct yourselves honorably among the Gentiles, so that when they slander you as evildoers, they will observe your good works and will glorify God on the day he visits. (1 Peter 2:12)

But if our gospel is veiled, it is veiled to those who are perishing. In their case, the god of this age has blinded the minds of the unbelievers to keep them from seeing the light of the gospel of the glory of Christ, who is the image of God. For we are not proclaiming ourselves but Jesus Christ as Lord, and ourselves as your servants for Jesus's sake. For God who said, "Let light shine out of darkness," has shone in our hearts to give the light of the knowledge of God's glory in the face of Jesus Christ. (2 Corinthians 4:3-6)

Unity

How good and pleasant it is when brothers live together in harmony! **(Psalm 133:1)**

Therefore I, the prisoner in the Lord, urge you to live worthy of the calling you have received, with all humility and gentleness, with patience, bearing with one another in love, making every effort to keep the unity of the Spirit through the bond of peace. **(Ephesians 4:1-3)**

Now the entire group of those who believed were of one heart and mind, and no one claimed that any of his possessions was his own, but instead they held everything in common. **(Acts 4:32)**

... make my joy complete by thinking the same way, having the same love, united in spirit, intent on one purpose. **(Philippians 2:2)**

Now I urge you, brothers and sisters, in the name of our Lord Jesus Christ, that all of you agree in what you say, that there be no divisions among you, and that you be united with the same understanding and the same conviction. **(1 Corinthians 1:10)**

Dale Evrist

Dale Evrist is a pastor and citywide ministry leader whose life's work has been dedicated to disciple-making. He is the Founding/Senior Pastor of New Song Nashville, a church and ministry committed to citywide disciple-making in partnership with the greater body of Christ. In addition to being a co-author of the *Kids Daily Life Journal*, he is also a co-author of the books in the *CORE4 Series,* the author of *The Mighty Hand of God,* and co-author of *Lifebook* with Dr. David Shibley. One of Dale's main passions is to provide biblically-based resources that equip Christ's church to see souls saved and disciples made.

Joel Evrist

Joel Evrist is a pastor, dynamic Bible teacher and proven disciple-maker with New Song Nashville, a church and ministry committed to citywide disciple-making in partnership with the greater body of Christ. In addition to being a co-author of the *Kids Daily Life Journal*, he is also a co-author of the books in the *CORE4 Series* and has written children's Bible study curriculum for LifeWay Christian Resources. Joel's greatest passion is making disciples who fully follow Jesus and teach others to do the same.

Donna Phillips

Donna Phillips is a pastor to the next generation and serves as an Associate Pastor at New Song Nashville, a church and ministry committed to citywide disciple-making in partnership with the greater body of Christ. In addition to being a co-author of the *Kids Daily Life Journal*, she has an extensive history ministering in a pastoral role to kids. Donna's greatest passion is to see kids saved, discipled and empowered by the Holy Spirit to live as overcoming believers while standing for righteousness in their generation.

Made in the USA
Columbia, SC
08 December 2019

84536733R00111